MODERN
ENGLISH ESSAYS

EDITED BY ERNEST RHYS

MODERN
ENGLISH ESSAYS
VOLUME THREE

"Q"
A.H.BULLEN
VERNON LEE
G. W. E. RUSSELL
MAX BEERBOHM
T. WATTS-DUNTON
GEORGE SAINTSBURY
J. ADDINGTON SYMONDS
AUGUSTINE BIRRELL
RICHARD JEFFERIES
WILLIAM ARCHER
VISCOUNT BRYCE
ANDREW LANG
MRS. MEYNELL
W.E. HENLEY
W.B.YEATS

1922

LONDON & TORONTO
J. M. DENT & SONS LTD.
NEW YORK: E. P. DUTTON & CO.

EDITOR'S NOTE

" I LOVE a man that doth stoutly express himself,"
said Montaigne, and his preference might well
point to the stout comments of W. E. Henley on
Hazlitt the essayist that give backbone to this
volume. Henley led at the close of last century a
little phalanx of his own, and made of *The Scots*
(that became *The National*) *Observer* (1889–1894)
another in the long succession of journals that
fostered the essay. His account of Hazlitt comes,
however, not from that source, but from an edition
of Hazlitt's works.

It may be placed with Augustine Birrell's account
of Lamb, also from a new edition of a favourite
author, in that series of justificative pieces on which
essayists rest their case for an independent canon.
Of their near contemporaries, Richard Jefferies is
a little master among the essayists of nature. " The
Sun and the Brook " comes from a posthumous
collection entitled *The Hills and the Vale*. Mrs.
Meynell, individual in her method as any of this
group, was a *National Observer* contributor who
had a pen sensitive and sure. She and " Vernon
Lee " (Miss Paget) have both written delightfully,
in their different ways, on the power and spirit
of place. The essay " Genius Loci " is from the
volume of that name. Mrs. Meynell's " Point
of Biography " is from her Collected Essays.

EDITOR'S NOTE

Among the recognised veterans of the critical essay at the century's close included in this group, John Addington Symonds, Andrew Lang, the late Lord Bryce, George Saintsbury, the late A. H. Bullen, and the sometime oracle of *The Athenæum*, Theodore Watts-Dunton, serve to knit up the late Victorian and the next generation. William Archer on Dr. Brandes and his *Shakespeare* marks in the account the place of the stage-critic as essayist. A causerie on the death of Robert Louis Stevenson (1894), by A. T. Q.-C., recalls the days when *The Speaker*, eventually merged in *The Nation*, was hospitable to new writers. W. B. Yeats was another of its contributors with a rare Celtic fantasy to maintain. His essay comes from an early volume of Irish folk-tales which he collected for the present editor many years ago. As for Max Beerbohm, wise and witty and joyously satirical by turns, he gave the essay a new commission in gaiety when he began, where other people end, by collecting his Works in a first book. In the same year (1896), let us recall, appeared his *Caricatures of Twenty-five Gentlemen*. The essays on *Joseph Andrews*, *Wild Wales*, *Peter Wilkins* and Abraham Lincoln are from the volumes of " Everyman's Library." Andrew Lang's Walton essay is from an edition of the *Compleat Angler* (1896).

E. R.

For permission to use copyright essays in this volume, special acknowledgments are due to Mr. Duckworth for the essay by Richard Jefferies; to Mrs. Meynell and Messrs. Burns and Oates for " A Point of Biography "; to Miss Paget ("Vernon Lee ") and Mr. John Lane for " Genius Loci "; to the Executors of the Walter Scott Co. for J. Addington Symonds' essay on the *Religio Medici*; and for Mr. W. B. Yeats' " Irish Folk and Fairy Tales "; to which should be added that poet and essayist's own consent.

To Sir Arthur T. Quiller-Couch, and to Messrs. Cassell and Co., the publishers are indebted for permission to use the essay on the Death of R. L. Stevenson; to Mr. William Archer and Mr. Grant Richards for that on Dr. Brandes' *Shakespeare*; and to Mr. Max Beerbohm, Mr. John Lane and Messrs. Dodd, Mead and Co. for " A Cloud of Pinafores." The other copyright items are reprinted from books in Messrs. Dent's own list of publications.

CONTENTS

MODERN ENGLISH ESSAYS

WILLIAM HAZLITT

By W. E. Henley

IT is told of him that he was dark-eyed and dark-haired, slim in figure, rather slovenly in his habit; that he valued himself on his effect in evening dress; that his manners were rather ceremonious than easy; that he had a wonderfully eloquent face, with a mouth as expressive as Kean's, and a frown like the Giaour's own [1]—that Giaour whom he did not love. He worshipped women, but was awkward and afraid with them; he played a good game of fives, and would walk his forty to fifty miles a day; he would lie abed till two in the afternoon, then rise, dally with his breakfast until eight without ever moving from his tea-pot and his chair, and go to a theatre, a bite at the Southampton, and talk till two in the morning.[2] That he excelled

---

[1]   There was a laughing devil in his sneer
      That raised emotions both of rage and fear;
      And where his frown of hatred darkly fell,
      Hope, withering, fled—and Mercy sighed farewell.

[2] These details are Patmore's, and, even if they be true, are not the whole truth. Hazlitt loved solitude and the country, had to write for a living, wrote with difficulty, and left no inconsiderable body of work.

in talk is beyond all doubt. Witness after witness is here to his wit, his insight, his grip on essentials, his beautiful trick of paradox, his brilliancy in attack, his desperate defence, his varying, far-glancing, inextinguishable capacity for expression. And he was himself—Hazlitt: a man who borrowed nobody's methods, set no limits to the field of discussion, nor made other men wonder if this were no talk but a lecture. He bore no likeness to that "great but useless genius," Coleridge: who, beginning well as few begin, lived ever after "on the sound of his own voice"; none to Wordsworth, whose most inspiring theme was his own poetry; none to Sheridan, who "never oped his mouth but out there flew" a jest; none to Lamb, who—— But no; I cannot imagine Lamb in talk. Hazlitt himself has plucked out only a tag or two of Lamb's mystery; and I own that, even in the presence of the notes in which he sets down Lamb as Lamb was to his intimates, I am divided in appreciation between the pair. Lamb for the unexpected, the incongruous, the profound, the jest that bred seriousness, the pun that was that and a light upon dark places, a touch of the dread, the all-disclosing Selene, besides; Hazlitt for none of these but for himself; and what that was I have tried to show. Well; Lamb, Coleridge, Sheridan, Hazlitt, Hunt, Wordsworth—all are dead, tall men of their tongues as they were. And dead is Burke, and Fox is dead, and Byron, most quizzical of lords! And of them all there is nothing left but their published work; and of those that have told us most about some of them, "in their habit as they lived," the best and the strictest-seeing, the most eloquent and the most persuasive, is assuredly Hazlitt. And, being something of an expert in talk,[1] I think that, if I could break the grave and call the great ghosts back to earth for a spell of their mortal fury, I would begin and end with Lamb and Hazlitt: Lamb as he always was;[2] Hazlitt in one of his high and mighty moods, sweeping life, and letters, and the art of painting, and the nature of man, and the curious case of woman (especially the curious case of woman!) into a rapture of give-and-take, a night-long series of achievements in consummate speech.

Many men, as Coleridge, have written well, and yet talked better than they wrote. I have named Coleridge, though his talk, prodigious as it was, in the long run ended in "Om-m-mject" and "Sum-m-mject," and though, some enchanting and undying verses apart, his writing, save when

---

[1] What I mean is, that I have heard the best, as I believe, the last of the old century and the first of the new have shown.

[2] "He always made the best pun and the best remark in the course of the evening. His serious conversation, like his serious writing, is his best. No one ever stammered out such fine, piquant, deep, eloquent things in half a dozen half-sentences as he does. His jests scald like tears: and he probes a question with a play upon words. What a keen, laughing, hare-brained vein of home-felt truth! What choice venom!"

it is merely critical, is nowadays of small account.
But, in truth, I have in my mind, rather, two
friends, both dead, of whom one, an artist in letters,
lived to conquer the English-speaking world, while
the second, who should, I think, have been the
greater writer, addicted himself to another art,
took to letters late in life, and, having the largest
and the most liberal utterance I have known, was
constrained by the very process of composition so to
produce himself that scarce a touch of his delightful,
apprehensive, all-expressing spirit appeared upon his
page. I take these two cases because both are
excessive. In the one you had both speech and
writing; in the other you found a rarer brain, a
more fanciful and daring humour, a richer gusto,
perhaps a wider knowledge, in any event a wider
charity. And at one point the two met, and that
point was talk. Therein each was pre-eminent,
each irresistible, each a master after his kind, each
endowed with a full measure of those gifts that
qualify the talker's temperament: as voice and
eye and laugh, look and gesture, humour and
fantasy, audacity and agility of mind, a lively and
most impudent invention, a copious vocabulary, a
right gift of foolery, a just, inevitable sense of
conversational right and wrong. Well; one wrote
like an angel, the other like poor Poll; and both
so far excelled in talk that I can take it on me to
say that they who know them only in print scarce
know them at all. 'Twas thus, I imagine, with
Hazlitt. He wrote the best he could; but I see

many reasons to believe that he was very much more brilliant and convincing at the Southampton than he is in the most convincing and the most brilliant of his Essays. He was a full man; he had all the talker's gifts; he exulted in all kinds of oral opportunities; what more is there to say? Sure 'tis the case of all that are born to talk as well as write. They live their best in talk, and what they write is but a sop for posterity: a last dying speech and confession (as it were) to show that not for nothing were they held rare fellows in their day.

This is not to say that Hazlitt was not an admirable man of letters. His theories were many, for he was a reality among men, and so had many interests, and there was none on which he did not write forcibly, luminously, arrestingly. He had the true sense of his material, and used the English language as a painter his pigments, as a musician the varying and abounding tonalities that constitute a symphonic scheme. His were a beautiful and choice vocabulary, an excellent ear for cadence, a notable gift of expression. In fact, when Stevenson was pleased to declare that " we are mighty fine fellows, but we cannot write like William Hazlitt," he said no more than the truth. Whether or not we are mighty fine fellows is a Great Perhaps; but that none of us, from Stevenson down, can as writers come near to Hazlitt—this, to me, is merely indubitable. To note that he now and then writes blank verse is to note that he sometimes

writes impassioned prose; [1] he misquoted habitually;
he was a good hater, and could be monstrous unfair;
he was given to thinking twice, and his second
thoughts were not always better than his first; he
repeated himself as seemed good to him. But in
the criticism of politics, the criticism of letters,
the criticism of acting, the criticism and expression
of life,[2] there is none like him. His politics are not

[1] It filled the valley like a mist,
    And still poured out its endless chant,
    And still it swells upon the ear,
    And wraps me in a golden trance,
    Drowning the noisy tumult of the world.

    .   .   .   .   .

    Like sweetest warblings from a sacred grove . . .
    Contending with the wild winds as they roar . . .
    And the proud places of the insolent
    And the oppressor fell . . .
    Such and so little is the mind of Man!

[2] His summary of the fight between Hickman and Bill
Neate is alone in literature, as also in the annals of the
Ring. Jon Bee was an intelligent creature of his kind,
and knew a very great deal more about pugilism than
Hazlitt knew; but to contrast the two is to learn much.
Badcock (which is Jon Bee) had seen (and worshipped)
Jem Belcher, and had reported fights with an extreme
contempt for Pierce Egan, the illiterate ass who gave us
Boxiana. Hazlitt, however, looked on at the proceedings
of Neate and the Gaslight Man exactly as he had looked
on at divers creations of Edmund Kean. He saw the
essentials in both expressions of human activity, and his
treatment of both is fundamentally the same. In both
he ignores the trivial: here the acting (in its lowest sense),
there the hits that did not count. And thus, as he gives
you only the vital touches, you know how and why Neate
beat Hickman, and can tell the exact moment at which
Hickman began to be a beaten man. 'Tis the same with
his panegyric on Cavanagh, the fives-player. For a blend

mine; I think he is ridiculously mistaken when
he contrasts the Wordsworth of the best things
in *The Excursion* with the " classic Akenside ";
his *Byron* is the merest petulance; his *Burke* (when
he is in a bad temper with Burke), his *Fox*, his *Pitt*,
his *Bonaparte*—these are impossible. Also, I never
talk art or life with him but I disagree. But I go
on reading him, all the same; and I find that
technically and spiritually I am always the better
for the bout. Where outside Boswell is there better
talk than in Hazlitt's " Boswell Redivivus "—his
so-called *Conversations with Northcote* ? And his
Age of Elizabeth, and his *Comic Writers*, and his
Spirit of the Age—where else to look for such a
feeling for differences, such a sense of literature,
such an instant, such a masterful, whole-hearted
interest in the marking and distinguishing qualities
of writers? And *The Plain Speaker*—is it not at
least as good reading as (say) *Virginibus Puerisque*
and the discoursings of the late imperishable Mr.

of gusto with understanding I know but one thing to
equal with this: the note on Dr. Grace, which appeared
in *The National Observer*; and the night that that was
written, I sent the writer back to Hazlitt's *Cavanagh*,
and said to him ——! On the whole the *Dr. Grace* is the
better of the two. But it has scarce the incorruptible
fatness of the *Cavanagh*. Gusto, though, is Hazlitt's
special attribute: he glories in what he likes, what he
reads, what he feels, what he writes. He triumphed in
his Kean, his Shakespeare, his Bill Neate, his Rousseau,
his coffee-and-cream and *Love for Love* in the inn-parlour
at Alton. He relished things; and expressed them with
a relish. That is his " note." Some others have relished
only the consummate expression of nothing.

Pater! His *Political Essays* is readable after—how many years? His notes on Kean and the Siddons are as novel and convincing as when they were penned. In truth, he is ever a solace and a refreshment. As a critic of letters he lacks the intense, immortalising vision, even as he lacks, in places, the illuminating and inevitable style of Lamb. But if he be less savoury, he is also more solid, and he gives you phrases, conclusions, splendours of insight and expression, high-piled and golden essays in appreciation: as the *Wordsworth* and the *Coleridge* of the *Political Essays*, the character of Hamlet, the note on Shakespeare's style, the *Horne Tooke*, the *Cervantes*, the *Rousseau*, the *Sir Thomas Browne*, the *Cobbett*: that must ever be rated high among the possessions of the English mind.

As a writer, therefore, it is with Lamb that I would bracket him: they are dissimilars, but they go gallantly and naturally together—*par nobile fratrum*.[1] Give us these two, with some ripe

[1] Listen, else, to Lamb himself: " Protesting against much that he has written, and some things which he chooses to do; judging him by his conversation which I enjoyed so long, and relished so deeply; or by his books, in those places where no clouding passion intervenes, I should belie my own conscience if I said less than that I think W. H. to be, in his natural and healthy state, one of the wisest and finest spirits breathing. So far from being ashamed of that intimacy which was betwixt us, it is my boast that I was able for so many years to have preserved it entire; and I think I shall go to my grave without finding or expecting to find such another companion." Thus does one Royalty celebrate the kingship and enrich the immortality of another.

Cobbett, a volume of Southey, some Wordsworth, certain pages of Shelley, a great deal of the Byron who wrote letters, and we get the right prose of the time. The best of it all, perhaps, is the best of Lamb. But Hazlitt's, for different qualities, is so imminent and shining a second that I hesitate as to the pre-eminency. Probably the race is Lamb's. But Hazlitt is ever Hazlitt; and at his highest moments Hazlitt is hard to beat, and has not these many years been beaten.

SCOTT AND DUMAS

By George Saintsbury

I DO not think that observation, however widely she may extend and however narrowly she may concentrate her view, will find in the history of literature anything quite similar to the achievement of the Waverley Novels. Their uniqueness does not consist wholly, or from the present point of view even mainly, in the fact that for bulk, excellence, and rapidity of production combined they can probably challenge anything else in letters. That they can do this I am by no means disposed to deny. But the point of pre-eminence at present to be considered is the singular and miraculous fashion in which Sir Walter, taking a kind of writing which had, as we have seen, been tried, or at least tried *at*, for more than two thousand years, and which had never yet been got to run smoothly on its own lines to its own end, by one stroke effected what the efforts of those two millenniums had been bungling and baulking themselves over.

That *Waverley* itself is the ideal of an historical novel need not be contended; and I do not know that any intelligent devotee would contend for anything of the kind. It bears, especially in its earlier chapters, too many marks of the old false procedure; and that insipidity of the nominal hero, which is so constantly and not so unjustly charged against Scott, appears in it pretty strongly. His unworldly education and the flustering influence of the Blessed Bear do not wholly excuse Waverley even in so early a matter as the Balmawhapple Duel. We can hardly blame his brother officers for suspecting him of poltroonery; and he can only clear himself from the charge of being a coward by submitting to that of being a simpleton. And though it is by no means the case that, according to the stupid old rule of critics like Rymer, a hero must be always wise as well as always fortunate, always virtuous as well as always brave, yet the kinds of folly permitted to him are rather limited in number. It is worth while to dwell on this in order to show that what is most wonderful about *Waverley* is not its individual perfection as a work of art; though the Baron, the Bailie, the whole of the actual scenes after the war breaks out, and many other things and persons, exalt it infinitely above anything of the kind known earlier.

But the chief marvel, the real point of interest, is the way in which, after thousands of years of effort to launch one particular ship into one particular ocean, she at last slips as by actual miracle into the waves and sweeps out into the open sea. Exactly how this came about it may be impossible to point out with any exhaustive certainty. Some reasons why the thing had not been done before were given in the past paper; some why it was done at this hour and by this man may perhaps be given in the present. But we shall have to end by assigning at least a large share of the explanation to the formula that "Walter Scott made historical novels because there was in him the virtue of the historical novelist."

Nevertheless we can perhaps find out a little about the component parts of this virtue, a little more about the antecedents and immediate workings of it. The desiderata which have been referred to before—the wide knowledge of history, the affectionate and romantic interest in the past— Scott possessed in common with his generation, but in very much larger measure and more intense degree than most of its members. Nor was it probably of slight importance that when he commenced historical novelist he was a man well advanced in middle age, and not merely provided with immense stores of reading, and with very considerable practice in composition of many kinds, but also experienced in more than one walk of practical business, thoroughly versed in society from the highest to the lowest ranks, and lastly, which is a matter of great importance in all cases, master of a large portion of his own time. It had indeed for years pleased him—as it did afterwards, fortunately or unfortunately, to a still greater extent — to dispose of much of this leisure in literary labour; but it was in labour of his own choosing, and neither in taskwork nor in work necessary for bread-winning. The Sheriffdom and the Clerkship (least distressful of places) freed him from all cares of this kind, augmented as his revenues were by the extraordinary sums paid for his poems.

But the most happy predisposition or preparation to be found in his earlier career was beyond all doubt his apprenticeship, if the word seem not too unceremonious, to these poems themselves. Here indeed he had far less to originate than in the novels. From the dawn of literature the narrative romance had been written in verse, and from the dawn of literature it had been wont at least to give itself out as historical. I am not sure, however, that the present age, which, while it gives itself airs of being unjust to Scott's prose, is unjust in reality to his poetry, does not even here omit to recognise the full value of his innovations or improvements. Of most classical narrative poems (the *Odyssey* being perhaps the sole exception) the famous saying about Richardson, that if you read for the story you would hang yourself, is true enough. It is true to a great extent of Milton, to some extent even of Spenser, and of nearly all the great narrative poets of the Continent, except Ariosto, in whom it is rather the stories than the story, rather the endless flow of romantic and comic digression than the plot and characters, that attract us. As for the mediæval writers whom Scott more immediately followed, I believe I am in a considerable minority. I find them interesting for the story; but most people do not find them so, and I cannot but admit myself that their interest of this kind varies very much indeed, and is very seldom of the highest.

With Scott it is quite different. Any child who is good for anything knows why *The Lay of the Last Minstrel* was so popular. It was not merely or mainly because the form was novel and daring; for nearly a hundred years past that form has been as familiar as Pope's couplet was to our great-grandfathers. It was not merely (though it was partly) because the thing is interspersed with passages of delightful and undoubted poetry. It was because it was and is interesting as a story; because the reader wanted to know what became of Deloraine and the Goblin page, and the rest; because the incidents and the scenes attracted, excited, fixed attention. This was even more the case in *Marmion* (which moreover approaches the historical novel in verse more nearly still), and it never failed in any of the rest. It was, to take some of the least popular of all the poems, because Scott could tell an incident as he has told the vengeance of Bertram Risingham in *Rokeby*, because he could knit together the well-worn and world-old string of familiar trials and temptations as he has done in *The Bridal of Triermain*, that he made his fortune in verse. He had the secret of tale-telling and of adjusting tales to facts. He taught it to Byron and others, and he made the popularity of the thing.

The suitableness of verse, however, for the story as the story, and especially for the historical novel as the historical novel, is so far inferior to that of prose, and the difficulty of keeping up a series of fictions in verse is so immeasurably greater than that of doing the same thing in prose, that I am disposed to believe that *Waverley* would have appeared all the same if there had been no Byron, and no chance of dethronement. In fact, the historical novel had to be created, and Scott had to create it. He had learned—if so dull and deliberate a process as learning can be asserted of what seems to have been as natural and as little troublesome to him as breathing—to build the romantic structure, to decorate it with ornament of fact and fancy from the records of the past, to depict scenery and manners, to project character, even to some extent to weave dialogue And I do not know that there is any more remarkable proof of his literary versatility in general, and his vocation for the historical novel in particular, than the fact that the very fault of prose romances, especially those immediately preceding his own, was also one most likely to be encouraged by a course of poetical practice, and yet is one from which he is almost entirely free.

The Godwins and the Mrs. Radcliffes had perpetually offended, now by dialogue so glaringly modern that it was utterly out of keeping with their story and their characters, now by the adoption of the conventional stage jargon which is one of the most detestable lingos ever devised by man. With very rare exceptions Sir Walter completely avoids both these dangers. His conversation has not, indeed, that prominence in the method of his work which we shall find it possessing in the case of his great French follower. But it is for the most part full of dramatic suitableness, it is often excellently humorous or pathetic, and it almost always possesses in some degree the Shakespearean quality of fitting the individual and the time and the circumstances without any deliberate archaism or modernism. No doubt Scott's wide reading enabled him to do a certain amount of mosaic work in this kind. Few for instance, except those whose own reading is pretty wide in the plays and pamphlets of the seventeenth century, know how much is worked from them into *The Fortunes of Nigel* and *Woodstock*. But this dialogue is never mere mosaic. It has the quality which, already called Shakespearean, also belongs to men of such different kinds and orders of greatness from Scott's or Shakespeare's as, for instance, Goldsmith—the quality of humanity, independent of time.

Now this is of itself of such importance to the historical novelist, that it may be doubted whether any other kind of craftsman can find it more important. The laborious and uninspired attempt at fidelity to " *temp.* of tale " in language, is nearly as destructive of the equanimity proper to the reception of a novel, as is the perpetual irritation which glaring and tasteless anachronisms of speech excite. And it is not particularly easy to say whether this knack plays a greater part in the fashioning of the "Scotch novel," (as it used to be called, with an odd mixture of propriety and impropriety), than the other ingredients of plot, character, and description. In regard to plot, Scott was from one point of view a great and confessing sinner; from another, a most admirably justified one. Plot, in the strict sense, he never achieved, and very seldom even attempted to achieve it. It was only the other day that there was published for the first time a letter from his intimate friend and one of his best critics, Lady Louisa Stuart (who, to be sure, had literature in the blood of her), stigmatising, more happily perhaps than has ever been done since, Sir Walter's habit of "huddling up the cards and throwing them into the bag in his impatience for a new deal." It may almost be said that Scott never winds up a plot artfully; and the censure which he makes Captain Clutterbuck pass in the introduction to *The Fortunes of Nigel* is undoubtedly valid. When Peacock, in *Crotchet Castle*, made that very crotchety comparison of Scott to a pantomime librettist, he might at least have justified it by the extraordinary fondness of the novelist for a sort of transformation-scene which finishes everything off in a trice, and, as Dryden says of his hasty preacher,

Runs huddling to the benediction.

The powerful and pathetic scenes at Carlisle

and the delightful restoration of the Baron somewhat mask, in *Waverley* itself, the extreme and
rather improbable ease with which the hero's
pardon is extorted from a government and a general
rather prone to deal harshly than mildly with
technical traitors. I never could make out how, if
Sir Arthur Wardour's fortune was half so badly
dipped as we are given to understand, his son,
even with more assistance from Lovel than a young
man of spirit was likely to accept from his sister's
suitor, could have disengaged it at the end of *The
Antiquary*. It is true that this is the least historical
of all the novels, but the procedure is the same.
Diana and her father were most theatrically lucky,
and Clerk Jobson, and even Rashleigh, scoundrels
as both were, were astonishingly unlucky, at the
close of *Rob Roy*; and it is especially difficult to
understand why the attorney was struck off the
rolls for joining in the attempt to secure an attainted
person who subsequently got off by killing the
officers of the law in the execution of their duty.
One might go on with this sort of peddling criticism
right through the series, winding up with that
catastrophe of *Woodstock* where Cromwell's mercy
is even more out of character and more unlikely
than Cumberland's. Nor are these conclusions
the only point of the novels, as usually constructed,
where a stop-watch critic may blaspheme without
the possibility of at least technical refutation of his
blasphemies. Scott has a habit (due no doubt in
part to his rapid and hazardous composition) of

introducing certain characters and describing certain incidents with a pomp and prodigality of detail quite out of proportion to their real importance in the story. And even a person who would no more hesitate to speak disrespectfully of the Unities than of the Equator may admit that such an arrangement as that in *Rob Roy*, where something like a quarter of the book is taken up with the adventures of four-and-twenty hours, is not wholly artistic.

Yet for my part I hold that the defence made by the shadowy Author of *Waverley* in the Introduction aforesaid is a perfectly sound one, and that it applies with special propriety to the historical division of the novels, and with them to historical novels generally. The Captain's gibe, conveyed in an anecdote of "his excellent grandmother," shows that Scott (as he was far too shrewd not to do) saw the weak points as well as the strong of this defence. Indeed I am not sure that he quite saw the strength of the strongest of all. It was all very well to plead that he was only "trying to write with sense and spirit a few scenes unlaboured and loosely put together, but which had sufficient interest in them to amuse in one corner the pain of body; in another to relieve anxiety of mind; in a third place to unwrinkle a brow bent with the furrows of daily toil; in another to fill the place of bad thoughts and suggest better; in yet another to induce an idler to study the history of his country; in all, save where the perusal interrupted the discharge of serious duties, to furnish harmless amusement." But the Captain might, if he had ventured to take such a liberty with the author of his being, have answered: " But, sir, could not you amuse and relieve and unwrinkle and fill and induce and furnish, and all the rest on't, at the same time joining your flats a little more carefully ? "

The Eidolon with the blotted revise would have done better, argumentatively speaking, to have stuck to his earlier plea, that, following Smollett and Le Sage, he tried to write rather a " history of the miscellaneous adventures which befall an individual in the course of life, than the plot of a regular and concerted *epopœia*, where every step brings us nearer to the final catastrophe." For it so happens that this plea is much nearer to the special business and ends of the historical novelist than to those of the avowedly inventive writer. As a matter of fact, we do know that Smollett certainly, and suspect that Le Sage probably, wove a great deal of actual experience into their stories; while Fielding, who is in the passage cited contrasted with them, seems never to have incorporated incidents, and at most a few characters, such as those of his wife, Allen, and one or two more whom he drew mainly in outline. A man who thus keeps clear of the servitude of actual occurrence, communicating reality by the results of his observation of human nature and human life generally, can shape the ends of his story as well as rough-hew them. But the man who makes incident and adventure his first object, and in some cases at least draws them from actual records, is bound to allow himself a licence much greater than epic strictness permits. That truth is stranger than fiction is only the copybook form of a reflection which a hundred critics have made and enforced in different ways since a thousand writers put the occasion before them—to wit, that in real life things happen in a more remiss and disorderly fashion than is allowable in fiction.

This point is indeed put very well by Scott himself in the introduction to *The Abbot*: " For whatever praise may be due to the ingenuity which brings to a general combination all the loose threads of a narrative, like the knitter at the finishing of her stocking, I am greatly deceived if in many cases a superior advantage is not attained by the air of reality which the deficiency of explanation attaches to a work written on a different system. In life itself many things befall every mortal of which the individual never knows the real cause or origin; and were we to point out the most marked distinction between a real and a fictitious narrative, we would say that the former in reference to the remote causes of the events it relates is obscure, doubtful, and mysterious, whereas in the latter case it is a part of the author's duty to afford satisfactory details upon the causes of the events he has recorded, and, in a word, to account for everything."

The historical novel, however, escapes this stricture in part because there the irregularities, the unexpectednesses, the disproportions of action,

are things accepted and not to be argued about.
Certain well-attested points and contrasts in the
character and conduct of Marlborough and of
Catherine the Second might be justly objected to
as unnatural in fiction: such historical incidents
as Clive's defence of Arcot, or as the last fight of
the *Revenge*, would at least be frowned or smiled
at as if they were mere inventions. Dealing as
the historical novelist must with actual and authenticated things like these, and moulding, as he will
if he is a deacon in his craft, his fictitious incidents
on their pattern, and to suit them, he can take to
himself all the irregularity, all the improbability,
all the outrages on the exact scale of Bossu, in
which life habitually indulges. And he is not
obliged—he is even decidedly unwise if he attempts
it—to adjust these things to theory and probability
by elaborate analyses of character. That is not
his business at all: he not only may, but should,
leave it to quite a different kind of practitioner.
His is the big brush, the bold foreshortening, the
composition which is all the more effective according as it depends least upon over-subtle strokes
and shades of line and colour. Not that he is to
draw carelessly or colour coarsely, but that niggling
finish of any kind is unnecessary and even pre-
judicial to his effects. And in the recognition, at
least in the practical recognition, of these laws of the
craft, as Scott set the example, so he also left very
little for any one else to improve upon. He may
have been equalled; he has never been surpassed.

I have before now referred by anticipation to another point of his intuition, his instinctive grasp of the first law of the historical novel, that the nominal hero and heroine, the ostensibly central interest and story shall not be or concern historical persons, or shall concern them only in some aspect unrecorded or at best faintly traced in history. The advantages of this are so clear and obvious that it is astounding that they should have been overlooked as they were, not merely by 'prentices of all kinds and all times, but by persons of something more than moderate ability like G. P. R. James and others. These advantages have been partly touched upon, but one of them has not, I think, been mentioned, and it may introduce to us another very important feature of the subject. It is constantly useful, and it may at times be indispensable, for the historical novelist to take liberties with history. The extent to which this is permissible or desirable may indeed be matter for plentiful disagreement. It is certainly carrying matters too far to make, as in *Castle Dangerous*, a happy ending to a story the whole historical and romantic complexion of which required the ending to be unhappy; but Sir Walter was admittedly but the shadow of himself when *Castle Dangerous* was written. Although Dryasdust and Smelfungus have both done after their worst fashion in objecting to his anachronisms in happier days, yet I certainly think that it was not necessary to make Shakespeare the author of *Midsummer Night's*

Dream in the eleventh year of his age, if not earlier, as is done in *Kenilworth,* or to play the tricks with chronology required by the narrative of the mis- deeds of Ulrica in *Ivanhoe.* Nothing is gained in either of these cases for the story. But there are cases where the story does undoubtedly gain by taking liberties with history. And it is evident that this can be done much more easily and much more effectively when the actual historical char- acters whose life is, so to speak, " coted and marked," do not play the first parts as far as the interest of the story goes.

But it might be tedious to examine more in detail the special characteristics of work so well known. Enough must have been said to show that Scott had discovered, and to a great extent had discovered consciously, not merely how to write an historical novel, but how to teach others to write it. His critical faculty, if not extraordinarily subtle, was always as sound and shrewd as it was good- natured. And there is hardly a better, as there is not a more interesting, example of this combination than the remarks in the " Diary " under the dates of October 17th and 18th, 1826, occasioned by Harrison Ainsworth's and Horace Smith's attempts in his style—*Sir John Chiverton* and *Brambletye House.* In one so utterly devoid of the slightest tendency to over-value himself, his adoption of Swift's phrase,

> Which I was born to introduce,
> Refined it first and shewed its use,

is a very strong affidavit of claim; and it is one which, as we have seen, is absolutely justified. Not less so are the remarks which follow a little later, on what he calls, with his unfailing *epieikeia*, his " own errors, or, if you will, those of the style." " One advantage," he says, " I think I still have over all of them. They may do it with a better grace, but I do it more naturally." And then in a succession of light taps with the finger he indicates not a few of the faults of the worst sort of historical novel: the acquiring information in order to write, instead of using in an unconstrained fashion what has become part of the regular furniture of the mind; the dragging in historical events by head and shoulders; the too open stealing of actual passages and pages from chronicles or previous works on the subject, and so forth; though he ends up with his usual honesty by confessing once more his own occasional carelessness of the management of the story.

He did not consider that his own plea of being " hurried on so that he has no time to think of the story " is a great deal more than an excuse. There is extremely little danger of much fault being found, except by professional fault-finders, with any writer who neglects the conduct of his story because he has so much story to tell. It is the other people, the people who are at their wits' end to know what ought to come next, who are intolerable, not those who have such an abundance of arrows in their quiver that they sometimes pull out one the notch of which does not exactly fit the string. I remember reading Mr. Crockett's *The Raiders*—one of the best of those books, which have been recently written in the more or less direct following of Scott—when it first appeared. I had to read it " in the way of business " (as Mr. Turnbull would say), and I soon saw that in the way of business there were many things that might be said against it. It was here and there too like this thing and that thing; its parts did not hang very well together; there were improbabilities not a few, and the crowning incident was not a little wanting in reason. But, having noted down these things duly, I turned to the beginning of the book once more and read it straight through, every word of it, a second time for my own private and unprofessional delectation. And I should suppose that the same thing must have happened and happened often to critics between 1815 and 1830.

For who can ever praise enough, or read enough, or enjoy enough, those forty-eight volumes of such a reader's paradise as nowhere else exists? The very abundance and relish of their pure delightsomeness has obscured in them qualities which would have made a score of reputations. Of passion there may be little or none; that string in Scott's case, as in those of Bacon, of Milton, of Southey, and others, was either wanting, or the artist's hand shrank from playing on it. But there is almost everything else. I once began, and mislaid, a collection of what would be called in our modern

jargon " realist " details from Scott, which showed
as shrewd a knowledge at least and as uncom-
promising an acknowledgment of the weaknesses
of human nature as with a little jargon and a little
brutality would have set up half a dozen psychological novelists.[1] In the observation and delineation
of his own countrymen he is acknowledged to have
excelled all other writers; by which I do not
mean merely that no one has drawn Scotsmen as
he has, but that no one writer has drawn that
writer's countrymen as Scott has. And the consensus, I believe, of the best critics would put him
next to Shakespeare as a creator of individual
character of the miscellaneous human sort, however
far he may be below not merely Shakespeare but
Fielding, Thackeray, and perhaps Le Sage in a certain subtle intimacy of detail and a certain massive
completeness of execution. And all these gifts—
all these and many more—he put at the service of
the kind that he " was born to introduce," the kind
of the historical novel.

Although Alexandre Dumas had begun to write
years before Sir Walter Scott's death, he had not
at that time turned his attention to the novels
which have ranked him as second only to Sir

[1] Curiously enough, after writing the above, I came
across the following passage in a little-known but extraordinarily shrewd French critic of English literature,
Mr. Browning's friend M. Milsand. " Il y a plus de philosophie dans ses [Scott's] contes (quoique la philosophie
n'en soit pas le caractère saillant) que dans bon nombre
de romans philosophiques."

Walter himself in that department. Nor was he
by any means Scott's first French imitator. He
was busy on dramatic composition, in which,
though he never attained anything like Scott's
excellence in his own kind of poetry, he was nearly
as great an innovator in his own country and way.
Nor can it be doubted that this practice helped
him considerably in his later work, just as Scott's
poetry had helped him, and in particular that it
taught Dumas a more closely knit construction
and a more constant " eye to the audience " than
Scott had always shown. Not indeed that the
plots of Dumas, as plots, are by any means of
exceptional regularity. The crimes and punish-
ment of Milady may be said to communicate a
certain unity to *Les Trois Mousquetaires*, the
vengeance of Dantes to *Monte Cristo*, and other
things to others. But when they are looked at
from the strictly dramatic side, all more or less are
" chronicle plays " in the form of novels, rather
than novels; lengths of adventure prolonged or
cut short at the pleasure or convenience of the
writer rather than definite evolutions of a certain
definite scheme, which has got to come to an end
when the ball is fully unrolled. The advantage of
Dumas's dramatic practice shows itself most in
the business-like way in which at his best he works
by *tableaux*, connected, it may be, with each other
rather by sequence and identity of personages than
by strict causality, but each possessing a distinct
dramatic and narrative interest of its own, and so

enchaining the attention. There are episodes without end in Dumas; but there are comparatively few (at least in his best work) of the " loose ends," of the incidents, neither complete in themselves nor contributing anything in particular to the general story, to which Sir Walter pleads guilty, and which certainly are to be found in him.

Another point in which Dumas may be said to have improved, or at any rate alternated, upon Scott, and which also may, without impropriety, be connected with his practice for the stage, is the enormously increased part allotted to dialogue in his novels. Certainly Scott was not weak in dialogue; on the contrary, the intrinsic excellence of the individual speeches of his characters in humour, in truth to nature, in pathos, and in many other important points, is decidedly above the Frenchman's. But his dialogue plays a much smaller part in the actual evolution of the story. Take down at hazard three or four different volumes of Dumas from the shelf; open them, and run over the pages, noting of what stuff the letterpress is composed. Then do exactly the same with the same number of Scott. You will find that the number of whole pages, and still more the number of consecutive pages, wholly filled with dialogue, or variegated with other matter in hardly greater proportion than that of stage directions, is far larger in the French than in the English master. It is true that the practice of Dumas varies in this respect. In his latter books especially, in his less

good ones at all times, there is a much greater
proportion of solid matter. But then the reason
of this is quite obvious. He was here falling either
in his own person, or by proxy, into those very
practices of interpolating lumps of chronicle, and
laboriously describing historic incident and scene,
with which, in the passage above quoted, Scott
reproaches his imitators. But at his best Dumas
delighted in telling his tale as much as possible
through the mouths of his characters. In all his
most famous passages—the scene at the Bastion
Saint-Gervais in *Les Trois Mousquetaires*, the Vin
de Porto and its ushering scenes in *Vingt Ans Après*,
the choicest episodes of *Le Vicomte de Bragelonne*,
the crises of *La Reine Margot* and *Les Quarante-
Cinq*, the thing is always talked rather than narrated.
It is hardly fanciful to trace Dumas's preference
for heroes like D'Artagnan and Chicot to the fact
that they had it by kind to talk.

I do not know whether it is worth while to lay
much stress on another difference between Scott
and Dumas—the much greater length of the latter's
novels and his tendency to run them into series.
Scott only did the latter once, in the case of *The
Monastery* and *The Abbot*, while it was probably
more a determination that the British public should
like him yet, in his dealings with so tempting a
subject as the troubles of Queen Mary's reign,
than any inherent liking for the practice that
determined him to it in this case. Even if we
neglect the trilogy system, of which the adventures

of D'Artagnan and Chicot are the main specimens, the individual length of Dumas's books is much greater than that of Scott's. Putting such giants as *Monte Cristo* and the *Vicomte de Bragelonne* aside, *Vingt Ans Après* would make, I should think, at least two *Waverleys*, and *La Reine Margot* (one of the shortest) an *Ivanhoe* and a half. But this increase in length was only a return to old practices; for Scott himself had been a great shortener of the novel. To say nothing of the romances of chivalry and the later imitations of them, Le Sage, Richardson, Fielding, Smollett, Mrs. Radcliffe, had all in their chief work run to a length far exceeding what Sir Walter usually thought sufficient. But I rather doubt whether even Mademoiselle de Scudéry's proverbial prolixity much exceeds in any one instance the length of the *Vicomte de Bragelonne*.

That this length is pretty closely connected with the conversational manner just noticed cannot, I think, be doubted. There is nothing so endless as talk; and inasmuch as an hour's leisurely speech will fill some thirty octavo pages, valiant talkers like Miss Bates must deliver (though fortunately not in a form which abides with posterity) their volume a day, year in and year out, given health and listeners, without any difficulty or much exertion. That is three hundred and sixty-five volumes a year, whereas five were all that even Southey's brazen-bowelled industry warranted itself to produce; and I do not think that Sir Walter himself in his most tremendous bursts of energy exceeded the rate of about a dozen.

Of the advantages and disadvantages, on the other hand, of the length thus reintroduced into novel-writing, it is not possible to speak with equal confidence. People who read very fast, who like to read more than once, and who are pleased to meet old friends in constantly new situations, as a rule, I think, like long books; but the average subscriber to circulating libraries does not. The taste for them is perhaps the more generous as it certainly is the most ancient and most human. It showed itself in the cycles of the ancients and of mediæval romance: it positively revelled in the extraordinary filiations of the *Amadis* story; and it has continued to assert itself in different forms to the present day, now in that of long single books, now in that of direct series and continuations, now in that of books like Thackeray's and Trollope's, which are not exactly series, but which keep touch with each other by the community of more or fewer characters. Of course it is specially easy to tempt and indulge this taste in the historical department of novel-writing. Even as it is, Dumas himself has made considerable progress in the task of writing a connected novel-history of France from the English wars to the Revolution of 1789. I really do not know that, especially now when the taste for the romance seems to have revived somewhat vigorously, it would be an inconceivable thing if somebody should write an English historical

Amadis in more than as many generations as the original, deducing the fortunes of an English family from King Arthur to Queen Victoria. Let it be observed that I do not as a critic recommend this scheme, nor do I specially hanker after its results as a reader. But it is not an impossible thing, and it would hardly exceed the total of Dumas's printed work. I have never been able to count that mighty list of volumes twice with the same result, a phenomenon well known in legend respecting the wonderful works of nature or of art. But it comes, I think, to somewhere about two hundred and forty volumes; that is to say, a hundred and twenty novels of the length of *Les Trois Mousquetaires* or *La Reine Margot*. And as that would cover the time suggested, at not more than ten or twelve years to a novel, it should surely be ample.

To return to a proper seriousness: the main points of strictly technical variation in Dumas as compared with Scott are thus the more important use made of dialogue, the greater length of the stories, and the tendency to run them on in series. In quality of enjoyment, also, the French master added something to his English model. If Scott is not deep (I think him much deeper than it is the fashion to allow), Dumas is positively superficial. His rapid and absorbing current of narrative gives no time for any strictly intellectual exertion on the part either of writer or reader; the style as style is even less distinct and less distinguished than Scott's; we receive not only few ideas but even few images of anything but action—few pictures of scenery, no extraordinarily vivid touches of customs or manners. Dumas is an infinitely inferior master of character to Scott; he can make up a personage admirably, but seldom attains to a real character. Chicot himself and Porthos are the chief exceptions; for D'Artagnan is more a type than an individual, Athos is the incarnate gentleman chiefly, Aramis is incomplete and shadowy, and Monte Cristo is a mere creature of melodrama.

But Dumas excels Scott himself in the peculiar and sustained faculty by which he can hold his reader by and for the story. With Sir Walter one is never quite unconscious, and one is delighted to be conscious, of the existence and individuality of the narrator. The " architect, artist, and man " (may Heaven forgive me, as Scott certainly would, for coupling his idea in any way with that of the subject of this phrase!) is always more or less before us, with his vast, if not altogether orderly, reading, his ardent patriotism, his saturation with romance coexisting with the shrewdest common-sense and knowledge of business, above all that golden temperament which made him a man of letters without pedantry and without vanity, a man of the world without frivolity and without guile, a " man of good " without prudery and without goodiness.

Of Dumas's personality (and no doubt this is in a way a triumph of his art) we never think at all.

We think of nothing but of the story: whether D'Artagnan will ever bring the diamonds safe home; whether the compact between Richelieu and Milady can possibly be fulfilled; whether that most terrible of all " black strap " that flowed into the pewter pot when Grimaud tried the cask will do its intended duty or not; whether Margaret will be able to divert the silk cord in Alençon's hand from its destination on La Môle's neck. No doubt Scott has moments of the same arresting excitement; but they are not so much his direct object, and from the difference of his method they are not so prominent or so numerous or engineered in such a manner as to take an equally complete hold of the reader. No doubt the generation which as yet had not Scott affected to find similar moments in Mrs. Radcliffe; but oh! the difference to us of the moment when Emily draws aside the Black Veil, and the moment when the corpse of Mordaunt shoots above water with the moonlight playing on the gold hilt of the dagger! Dumas indeed has no Wandering Willie; he had not poetry enough in him for that. But in the scenes where Scott as a rule excels him—the scenes where the mere excitement of adventure is enhanced by nobility of sentiment—he has a few, with the death of Porthos at the head of them, which are worthy of Scott himself; while of passages like the famous rescue of Henry Morton from the Cameronians he has literally hundreds.

It was, then, this strengthening and extending

of the absorbing and exciting quality which the
historical novel chiefly owed to Dumas, just as
it owed its first just and true concoction and the
indication of almost all the ways in which it could
seek perfection to Scott. I shall not, I think, be
charged with being unjust to the pupil; but,
wonderful as his work is, I think it not so much
likely as certain that it never would have been
done at all if it had not been for the Master.

HENRY FIELDING AND "JOSEPH ANDREWS"

By George Saintsbury

THERE are few amusements more dangerous for an author than the indulgence in ironic descriptions of his own work. If the irony is depreciatory, posterity is but too likely to say, " Many a true word is spoken in jest "; if it is encomiastic, the same ruthless and ungrateful critic is but too likely to take it as an involuntary confession of folly and vanity. But when Fielding, in one of his serio-comic introductions to *Tom Jones*, described it as " this prodigious work," he all unintentionally (for he was the least pretentious of men) anticipated the verdict which posterity almost at once, and with ever-increasing suffrage of the best judges as time went on, was about to pass not merely upon this particular book, but upon his whole genius and his whole production as a novelist. His work in other kinds is of a very different order of excellence. It is sufficiently interesting at times in itself; and always more than sufficiently interesting as his. Until the present occasion came (which made it necessary that I should acquaint myself with it) I own that my own knowledge of these miscellaneous writings was by no means thorough. It is now pretty complete; but the idea which I previously had of them at first and second hand, though a little improved, has not very materially altered. Though in all this hack-work Fielding displayed, partially and at intervals, the same qualities which he displayed eminently and constantly in the four great books here given, he was not, as the French idiom expresses it, *dans son assiette*, in his own natural and impregnable disposition and situation of character and ability, when he was occupied on it. The novel was for him that *assiette*.

Although Henry Fielding lived in quite modern times, although by family and connections he was of a higher rank than most men of letters, and although his genius was at once recognised by his contemporaries so soon as it displayed itself in its proper sphere, his biography until very recently was by no means full; and the most recent researches, including those of Mr. Austin Dobson—a critic unsurpassed for combination of literary faculty and knowledge of the eighteenth century—have not altogether sufficed to fill up the gaps. His family, said to have descended from a member of the great house of Hapsburg who came to England in the reign of Henry II., distinguished itself in the Wars of the Roses, and in the seventeenth century was advanced to the peerages of Denbigh in England and (later) of Desmond in Ireland. The novelist was the grandson of John Fielding, Canon of Salisbury, the fifth son of the first Earl of Desmond of this creation. The canon's third son, Edmond, entered the army, served under Marlborough, and married Sarah Gold or Gould, daughter of a judge of the King's Bench. Their eldest son was Henry, who was born on 22nd April, 1707, and had an uncertain number of brothers and sisters of the whole blood. After his first wife's death, General Fielding (for he attained that rank) married again. The most remarkable offspring of the first marriage, next to Henry, was his sister Sarah, also a novelist, who wrote *David Simple*; of the second, John, afterwards Sir John Fielding, who, though blind, succeeded his half-brother as a Bow Street magistrate, and in that office combined an equally honourable record with a longer tenure.

Fielding was born at Sharpham Park in Somersetshire, the seat of his maternal grandfather; but most of his early youth was spent at East Stour in Dorsetshire, to which his father removed after the judge's death. He is said to have received his first education under a parson of the neighbourhood named Oliver, in whom a very uncomplimentary tradition sees the original of Parson Trulliber. He was then certainly sent to Eton, where he did not waste his time as regards learning, and made several valuable friends. But the dates of his entering and leaving school are alike unknown; and his subsequent sojourn at Leyden for two years—though there is no reason to doubt it—depends even less upon any positive documentary evidence. This famous University still had a great repute as a training school in law, for which profession he was intended; but the reason why he did not receive the even then far more usual completion of a public school education by a sojourn at Oxford or Cambridge may be suspected to be different. It may even have had something to do with a curious escapade of his about which not very much is known—an attempt to carry off a pretty heiress of Lyme, named Sarah Andrew.

Even at Leyden, however, General Fielding seems to have been unable or unwilling to pay his son's expenses, which must have been far less there than at an English University; and Henry's return to London in 1728-29 is said to have been due to sheer impecuniosity. When he returned to England, his father was good enough to make him an allowance of £200 nominal, which appears to have been equivalent to £0 actual. And as practically nothing is known of him for the next six or seven years, except the fact of his having worked industriously enough at a large number of not very good plays of the lighter kind, with a few poems and miscellanies, it is reasonably enough supposed that he lived by his pen. The only product of this period which has kept (or indeed which ever received) competent applause is *Tom Thumb, or the Tragedy of Tragedies*, a following of course of the *Rehearsal*, but full of humour and spirit. The most successful of his other dramatic works were the *Mock Doctor* and the *Miser*, adaptations of Molière's famous pieces. His undoubted connection with the stage, and the fact of the contemporary existence of a certain Timothy Fielding, helped suggestions of less dignified occupations as actor, booth-keeper, and so forth; but these have long been discredited and indeed disproved.

In or about 1735, when Fielding was twenty-eight, we find him in a new, a more brilliant and agreeable, but even a more transient phase. He had married (we do not know when or where) Miss Charlotte Cradock, one of three sisters who lived at Salisbury (it is to be observed that Fielding's entire connections, both in life and letters, are with the Western Counties and London), who were certainly of competent means, and for whose alleged illegitimacy there is no evidence but an unsupported fling of that old maid of genius, Richardson. The descriptions both of Sophia and of Amelia are said to have been taken from this lady; her good looks and her amiability are as well established as anything of the kind can be in the absence of photographs and affidavits; and it is certain that her husband was passionately attached to her, during their too short married life. His method, however, of showing his affection smacked in some ways too much of the foibles which he has attributed to Captain Booth, and of those which we must suspect Mr. Thomas Jones would also have exhibited, if he had not been adopted as Mr. Allworthy's heir, and had not had Mr. Western's fortune to share and look forward to. It is true that grave breaches have been made by recent criticism in the very picturesque and circumstantial story told on the subject by Murphy, the first of Fielding's biographers. This legend was that Fielding, having succeeded by the death of his mother to a small estate at East Stour, worth about £200 a year, and having received £1500 in ready money as his wife's fortune, got through the whole in three years by keeping open house, with a large retinue in "costly yellow liveries," and so forth. In details, this story has been simply riddled. His mother had died long before; he was certainly not away from London three years, or anything like it; and so forth. At the same time, the best and soberest judges agree that there is an intrinsic probability, a consensus (if a vague one) of tradition, and a chain of almost unmistakably personal references in the novels, which plead for a certain amount of truth, at the bottom of a much embellished legend. At any rate, if Fielding established himself in the country, it was not long before he returned to town; for early in 1736 we find him back again, and not merely a playwright, but lessee of the "Little Theatre" in the Haymarket. The plays which he produced here—satirico-political pieces, such as *Pasquin* and the *Historical Register*—were popular enough, but offended the Government; and in 1737 a new Bill regulating theatrical performances, and instituting the Lord Chamberlain's control, was passed. This measure put an end directly to the "Great Mogul's Company," as Fielding had called his troop, and indirectly to its manager's career as a playwright. He did indeed write a few pieces in future years, but they were of the smallest importance.

After this check he turned at last to a serious profession, entered himself of the Middle Temple in November of the same year, and was called three years later; but during these years, and indeed for some time afterwards, our information about him is still of the vaguest character. Nobody doubts that he had a large share in the *Champion*, an essay-periodical on the usual eighteenth-century model, which began to appear in 1739, and which is still occasionally consulted for the work that is certainly or probably his. He went the Western Circuit, and attended the Wiltshire Sessions, after he was called, giving up his contributions to periodicals soon after that event. But he soon returned to literature proper, or rather made his *début* in it, with the immortal book now republished. The *History of the Adventures of Joseph Andrews and his Friend Mr. Abraham Adams* appeared in February 1742, and its author received from Andrew Millar, the publisher, the sum of £183 11s. Even greater works have fetched much smaller sums; but it will be admitted that *Joseph Andrews* was not dear.

The advantage, however, of presenting a survey of an author's life uninterrupted by criticism is so clear, that what has to be said about *Joseph* may be conveniently postponed for the moment. Immediately after its publication the author fell back upon miscellaneous writing, and in the next year (1743) collected and issued three volumes of

Miscellanies. In the two first volumes the only thing of much interest is the unfinished and unequal, but in part powerful, *Journey from this World to the Next,* an attempt of a kind which Fontenelle and others, following Lucian, had made very popular with the time. But the third volume of the *Miscellanies* deserved a less modest and gregarious appearance, for it contained, and is wholly occupied by, the wonderful and terrible satire of *Jonathan Wild,* the greatest piece of pure irony in English out of Swift. Soon after the publication of the book, a great calamity came on Fielding. His wife had been very ill when he wrote the preface; soon afterwards she was dead. They had taken the chance, had made the choice, that the more prudent and less wise student-hero and heroine of Mr. Browning's *Youth and Art* had shunned; they had no doubt " sighed deep, laughed free, Starved, feasted, despaired," and we need not question, that they had also " been happy."

Except this sad event and its rather incongruous sequel, Fielding's marriage to his wife's maid Mary Daniel—a marriage, however, which did not take place till full four years later, and which by all accounts supplied him with a faithful and excellent companion and nurse, and his children with a kind stepmother—little or nothing is again known of this elusive man of genius between the publication of the *Miscellanies* in 1743 and that of *Tom Jones* in 1749. The second marriage itself in November 1747; an interview which Joseph Warton had

with him rather more than a year earlier (one of
the very few direct interviews we have); the publication of two anti-Jacobite newspapers (Fielding
was always a strong Whig and Hanoverian), called
the *True Patriot* and the *Jacobite's Journal,* in
1745 and the following years; some indistinct
traditions about residences at Twickenham and
elsewhere, and some, more precise but not much
more authenticated, respecting patronage by the
Duke of Bedford, Mr. Lyttelton, Mr. Allen, and
others, pretty well sum up the whole.

Tom Jones was published in February (a favourite
month with Fielding or his publisher Millar) 1749;
and as it brought him the, for those days, very
considerable sum of £600, to which Millar added
another hundred later, the novelist must have been,
for a time at any rate, relieved from his chronic
penury. But he had already, by Lyttelton's interest,
secured his first and last piece of preferment, being
made Justice of the Peace for Westminster, an
office on which he entered with characteristic
vigour. He was qualified for it not merely by a
solid knowledge of the law, and by great natural
abilities, but by his thorough kindness of heart;
and, perhaps, it may also be added, by his long years
of queer experience on (as Mr. Carlyle would have
said) the " burning marl " of the London Bohemia.
Very shortly afterwards he was chosen Chairman
of Quarter Sessions, and established himself in Bow
Street. The Bow Street magistrate of that time
occupied a most singular position, and was more

like a French Prefect of Police or even a Minister
of Public Safety than a mere justice. Yet he was
ill paid. Fielding says that the emoluments, which
before his accession had but been £500 a year of
" dirty " money, were by his own action but £300
of clean; and the work, if properly performed,
was very severe.

That he performed it properly all competent
evidence shows, a foolish, inconclusive, and I fear
it must be said emphatically snobbish story of
Walpole's notwithstanding. In particular, he broke
up a gang of cut-throat thieves, which had been
the terror of London. But his tenure of the post
was short enough, and scarcely extended to five
years. His health had long been broken, and he
was now constantly attacked by gout, so that he
had frequently to retreat on Bath from Bow Street,
or his suburban cottage of Fordhook, Ealing. But
he did not relax his literary work. His pen was
active with pamphlets concerning his office; *Amelia*,
his last novel, appeared towards the close of 1751;
and next year saw the beginning of a new paper,
the *Covent Garden Journal*, which appeared twice
a week, ran for the greater part of the year, and
died in November. Its great author did not see
that month twice again. In the spring of 1753 he
grew worse; and after a year's struggle with ill
health, hard work, and hard weather, lesser measures
being pronounced useless, was persuaded to try the
" Portugal Voyage," of which he has left so charming a record in the *Journey to Lisbon*. He left

Fordhook on 26th June, 1754, reached Lisbon in August, and, dying there on the 8th of October, was buried in the cemetery of the Estrella.

Of not many writers perhaps does a clearer notion, as far as their personality goes, exist in the general mind that interests itself at all in literature than of Fielding. Yet more than once a warning has been sounded, especially by his best and most recent biographer, to the effect that this idea is founded upon very little warranty of scripture. The truth is, that as the foregoing record—which, brief as it is, is a sufficiently faithful summary—will have shown, we know very little about Fielding. We have hardly any letters of his, and so lack the best by far and the most revealing of all character-portraits; we have but one important autobiographic fragment, and though that is of the highest interest and value, it was written far in the valley of the shadow of death, it is not in the least retrospective, and it affords but dim and inferential light on his younger, healthier, and happier days and ways. He came, moreover, just short of one set of men of letters, of whom we have a great deal of personal knowledge, and just beyond another. He was neither of those about Addison, nor of those about Johnson. No intimate friend of his has left us anything elaborate about him. On the other hand, we have a far from inconsiderable body of documentary evidence, of a kind often by no means trustworthy. The best part of it is contained in the letters of his cousin, Lady Mary Wortley Montagu, and the reminiscences or family traditions of her grand-daughter, Lady Louisa Stuart. But Lady Mary, vivacious and agreeable as she is, had with all her talent a very considerable knack of writing for effect, of drawing strong contrasts and the like; and it is not quite certain that she saw very much of Fielding in the last and most interesting third of his life. Another witness, Horace Walpole, to less knowledge and equally dubious accuracy, added decided ill-will, which may have been due partly to the shrinking of a dilettante and a fop from a burly Bohemian; but I fear is also consequent upon the fact that Horace could not afford to despise Fielding's birth, and knew him to be vastly his own superior in genius. We hear something of him again from Richardson; and Richardson hated him with the hatred of dissimilar genius, of inferior social position, and, lastly, of the cat for the dog who touzles and worries her. Johnson partly inherited or shared Richardson's aversion, partly was blinded to Fielding's genius by his aggressive Whiggery. I fear, too, that he was incapable of appreciating it for reasons other than political. It is certain that Johnson, sane and robust as he was, was never quite at ease before genius of the gigantic kind, either in dead or living. Whether he did not like to have to look up too much, or was actually unable to do so, it is certain that Shakespeare, Milton, Swift, and Fielding, those four Atlantes of English verse and prose, all affected him with luke-warm admiration, or with positive dislike, for which it is vain to attempt to assign any uniform secondary cause, political or other. It may be permitted to hint another reason. All Johnson's most sharp-sighted critics have noticed, though most have dis-creetly refrained from insisting on, his "thorn-in-the-flesh," the combination in him of very strong physical passions with the deepest sense of the moral and religious duty of abstinence. It is perhaps impossible to imagine anything more distasteful to a man so buffeted, than the extreme indulgence with which Fielding regards, and the easy freedom, not to say gusto, with which he depicts, those who succumb to similar temptation. Only by supposing the workings of some subtle influence of this kind is it possible to explain, even in so capricious a humour as Johnson's, the famous and absurd appli-cation of the term "barren rascal" to a writer who, dying almost young, after having for many years lived a life of pleasure, and then for four or five one of laborious official duty, has left work any-thing but small in actual bulk, and fertile with the most luxuriant growth of intellectual originality.

Partly on the *obiter dicta* of persons like these, partly on the still more tempting and still more treacherous ground of indications drawn from his works, a Fielding of fantasy has been constructed, which in Thackeray's admirable sketch attains real life and immortality as a creature of art, but which possesses rather dubious claims as a historical charac-ter. It is astonishing how this Fielding of fantasy sinks and shrivels when we begin to apply the horrid tests of criticism to his component parts. The *eidolon*, with inked ruffles and a towel round his head, sits in the Temple and dashes off articles for the *Covent Garden Journal*; then comes Criticism, hellish maid, and reminds us that when the *Covent Garden Journal* appeared, Fielding's wild oats, if ever sown at all, had been sown long ago; that he was a busy magistrate and householder in Bow Street; and that, if he had towels round his head, it was probably less because he had exceeded in liquor than because his Grace of Newcastle had given him a headache by wanting elaborate plans and schemes prepared at an hour's notice. Lady Mary, apparently with some envy, tells us that he could " feel rapture with his cook-maid." " Which many has," as Mr. Ridley remarks, from Xanthias Phoceus downwards; but when we remember the historic fact that he married this maid (not a " cook-maid " at all), and that though he always speaks of her with warm affection and hearty respect, such " raptures " as we have of his clearly refer to a very different woman, who was both a lady and a beautiful one, we begin a little to shake our heads. Horace Walpole at second-hand draws us a Fielding pigging with low companions in a house kept like a hedge tavern; Fielding himself, within a year or two, shows us more than half-undesignedly in the *Voyage to Lisbon* that he was very careful about the appointments and decency of his table, that he stood rather upon ceremony in regard to his own treatment of his family, and the treatment of them and himself by others, and that he was altogether a person orderly, correct, and even a little finikin. Nor is there the slightest reasonable reason to regard this as a piece of hypocrisy, a vice as alien from the Fielding of fancy as from the Fielding of fact, and one the particular manifestation of which, in this particular place, would have been equally unlikely and unintelligible.

It may be asked whether I propose to substitute for the traditional Fielding a quite different person, of regular habits and methodical economy. Certainly not. The traditional estimate of great men is rarely wrong altogether, but it constantly has a habit of exaggerating and dramatising their characteristics. For some things in Fielding's career we have positive evidence of document, and evidence hardly less certain of probability. Although I believe the best judges are now of opinion that his impecuniosity has been overcharged, he certainly had experiences which did not often fall to the lot of even a cadet of good family in the eighteenth century. There can be no reasonable doubt that he was a man who had a leaning towards pretty girls and bottles of good wine; and I should suppose that if the girl were kind and fairly winsome, he would not have insisted that she should possess Helen's beauty, that if the bottle of good wine were not forthcoming, he would have been very tolerant of a mug of good ale. He may very possibly have drunk more than he should, and lost more than he could conveniently pay. It may be put down as morally ascertained that towards all these

weaknesses of humanity, and others like unto them,
he held an attitude which was less that of the un-
assailable philosopher than that of the sympathiser,
indulgent and excusing. In regard more especially
to what are commonly called moral delinquencies,
this attitude was so decided as to shock some people
even in those days, and many in these. Just when
the first sheets of this edition were passing through
the press, a violent attack was made in a newspaper
correspondence on the morality of *Tom Jones* by
certain notorious advocates of Purity, as some say,
of Pruriency and Prudery combined, according to
less complimentary estimates. Even midway between
the two periods we find the admirable Miss Ferrier,
a sister of Fielding's own craft, who sometimes had
touches of nature and satire not far inferior to his
own, expressing by the mouth of one of her characters with whom she seems partly to agree, the
sentiment that his works are "vanishing like
noxious exhalations." Towards any misdoing by
persons of the one sex towards persons of the other,
when it involved brutality or treachery, Fielding
was pitiless; but when treachery and brutality were
not concerned, he was, to say the least, facile. So,
too, he probably knew by experience—he certainly
knew by native shrewdness and acquired observation—that to look too much on the wine when it
is red, or on the cards when they are parti-coloured,
is ruinous to health and fortune; but he thought
not over badly of any man who did these things.
Still it is possible to admit this in him, and to stop

short of that idea of a careless and reckless *viveur* which has so often been put forward. In particular, Lady Mary's view of his childlike enjoyment of the moment has been, I think, much exaggerated by posterity, and was probably not a little mistaken by the lady herself. There are two moods in which the motto is *Carpe diem*; one a mood of simply childish hurry, the other one where behind the enjoyment of the moment lurks, and in which the enjoyment of the moment is not a little heightened by, that vast ironic consciousness of the before and after, which I at least see everywhere in the background of Fielding's work.

The man, however, of whom we know so little, concerns us much less than the author of the works, of which it only rests with ourselves to know everything. I have above classed Fielding as one of the four Atlantes of English verse and prose, and I doubt not that both the phrase and the application of it to him will meet with question and demur. I have only to interject, as the critic so often has to interject, a request to the court to take what I say in the sense in which I say it. I do not mean that Shakespeare, Milton, Swift, and Fielding are in all or even in most respects on a level. I do not mean that the three last are in all respects of the greatest names in English literature. I only mean that, in a certain quality, which for want of a better word I have chosen to call Atlantean, they stand alone. Each of them, for the metaphor is applicable either way, carries a whole

world on his shoulders, or looks down on a whole
world from his natural altitude. The worlds are
different, but they are worlds; and though the
attitude of the giants is different also, it agrees in
all of them on the points of competence and strength.
Take whomsoever else we may among our men of
letters, and we shall find this characteristic to be in
comparison wanting. These four carry their world,
and are not carried by it; and if it, in the language
so dear to Fielding himself, were to crash and
shatter, the inquiry, " *Que vous reste-t-il ?* " could
be answered by each, " *Moi !* "

The appearance which Fielding makes is no
doubt the most modest of the four. He has not
Shakespeare's absolute universality, and in fact not
merely the poet's tongue, but the poet's thought
seems to have been denied him. His sphere is not
the ideal like Milton's. His irony, splendid as it is,
falls a little short of that diabolical magnificence
which exalts Swift to the point whence, in his own
way, he surveys all the kingdoms of the world,
and the glory or vainglory of them. All Fielding's
critics have noted the manner, in a certain sense
modest, in another ostentatious, in which he seems
to confine himself to the presentation of things
English. They might have added to the presentation of things English—as they appear in London,
and on the Western Circuit, and on the Bath Road.

But this apparent parochialism has never deceived
good judges. It did not deceive Lady Mary, who
had seen the men and manners of very many climes;

it did not deceive Gibbon, who was not especially prone to overvalue things English, and who could look down from twenty centuries on things ephemeral. It deceives, indeed, I am told, some excellent persons at the present day, who think Fielding's microcosm a "toylike world," and imagine that Russian Nihilists and French Naturalists have gone beyond it. It will deceive no one who has lived for some competent space of time a life during which he has tried to regard his fellow-creatures and himself, as nearly as a mortal may, *sub specie æternitatis*.

As this is in the main an introduction to Fielding's four great novels, the justification in detail of the estimate just made or hinted of the novelist's genius will be best and most fitly made by a brief discussion of the four as presented; and, indeed, it is not fanciful to perceive in each book a somewhat different presentment of the author's genius, though in no one of the four is any one of his masterly qualities absent. There is tenderness even in *Jonathan Wild*; there are touches in *Joseph Andrews* of that irony of the Preacher, the last echo of which is heard amid the kindly resignation of the *Journey to Lisbon*, in the sentence, "Whereas envy of all things most exposes us to danger from others, so contempt of all things best secures us from them." But on the whole it is safe to say that *Joseph Andrews* best presents Fielding's mischievous and playful wit; *Jonathan Wild* his half-Lucianic, half-Swiftian irony; *Tom Jones* his unerring knowledge of human nature, and his constructive faculty;

GEORGE SAINTSBURY

Amelia his tenderness, his *mitis sapientia*, his observation of the details of life. And first of the first.

   *The History of the Adventures of Joseph Andrews
and his Friend Mr. Abraham Adams* was, as has
been said above, published in February 1742. In
the agreement between author and publisher, it is
not uninteresting to observe that the witness,
William Young, is none other than the asserted
original of the immortal Mr. Adams himself. He
might, on Balzac's plea in a tolerably well-known
anecdote, have demanded half of the £183 11s.
Of the other origins of the book we have a pretty
full account, partly documentary. That it is " writ
in the manner of Cervantes," and is intended as a
kind of comic epic, is the author's own statement
—no doubt as near the actual truth as is consistent
with comic-epic theory. That there are resemblances to Scarron, to Le Sage, and to other practitioners of the Picaresque novel is certain; and it
was inevitable that there should be. Of directer
and more immediate models or starting-points one
is undoubted; the other, though less generally
admitted, not much less indubitable to my mind.
The parody of Richardson's *Pamela*, which was
little more than a year earlier (November 1740), is
avowed, open, flagrant; nor do I think that the
author was so soon carried away by the greater and
larger tide of his own invention as some critics
seem to hold. He is always more or less returning
to the ironic charge; and the multiplicity of the
assailants of Joseph's virtue only disguises the re-

56

semblance to the long-drawn dangers of Pamela from a single ravisher. But Fielding was also well acquainted with Marivaux's *Paysan Parvenu*, and the resemblances between that book and *Joseph Andrews* are much stronger than Fielding's admirers have always been willing to admit. This recalcitrance has, I think, been mainly due to the erroneous conception of Marivaux as, if not a mere fribble, yet a Dresden-Shepherdess kind of writer, good at "preciousness" and patch-and-powder manners, but nothing more. There was, in fact, a very strong satiric and ironic touch in the author of *Marianne*, and I do not think that I was too rash when some years ago I ventured to speak of him as " playing Fielding to his own Richardson " in the *Paysan Parvenu*.

Origins, however, and indebtedness and the like, are, when great work is concerned, questions for the study and the lecture-room, for the literary historian and the professional critic, rather than for the reader, however intelligent and alert, who wishes to enjoy a masterpiece, and is content simply to enjoy it. It does not really matter how close to anything else something which possesses independent goodness is; the very utmost technical originality, the most spotless purity from the faintest taint of suggestion, will not suffice to confer merit on what does not otherwise possess it. Whether, as I rather think, Fielding pursued the plan he had formed *ab incepto*, or whether he cavalierly neglected it, or whether the current of his own genius carried him off his legs and landed him, half against his will, on the shore of originality, are questions for the schools, and, as I venture to think, not for the higher forms in them. We have *Joseph Andrews* as it is; and we may be abundantly thankful for it. The contents of it, as of all Fielding's work in this kind, include certain things for which the moderns are scantly grateful. Of late years, and not of late years only, there has grown up a singular and perhaps an ignorant impatience of digressions, of episodes, of tales within a tale. The example of this which has been most maltreated is the " Man of the Hill " episode in *Tom Jones*; but the stories of the " Unfortunate Jilt " and of Mr. Wilson in our present subject do not appear to me to be much less obnoxious to the censure; and *Amelia* contains more than one or two things of the same kind. Me they do not greatly disturb; and I see many defences for them besides the obvious, and at a pinch suffi-cient one, that divagations of this kind existed in all Fielding's Spanish and French models, that the public of the day expected them, and so forth. This defence is enough, but it is easy to amplify and reintrench it. It is not by any means the fact that the Picaresque novel of adventure is the only or the chief form of fiction which prescribes or admits these episodic excursions. All the classical epics have them; many Eastern and other stories present them; they are common, if not invariable, in the abundant mediæval literature of prose and verse romance; they are not unknown by any means in the modern novel; and you will very rarely hear a story told orally at the dinner-table or in the smoking-room without something of the kind. There must, therefore, be something in them corresponding to an inseparable accident of that most unchanging of all things, human nature. And I do not think the special form with which we are here concerned by any means the worst that they have taken. It has the grand and prominent virtue of being at once and easily skippable. There is about Cervantes and Le Sage, about Fielding and Smollett, none of the treachery of the modern novelist, who induces the conscientious reader to drag through pages, chapters, and sometimes volumes which have nothing to do with the action, for fear he should miss something that has to do with it. These great men have a fearless frankness, and almost tell you in so many words when and what you may skip. Therefore, if the " Curious Impertinent," and the " Baneful Marriage," and the " Man of the Hill," and the " Lady of Quality," get in the way, when you desire to " read for the story," you have nothing to do but turn the page till *finis* comes. The defence has already been made by an illustrious hand for Fielding's inter-chapters and exordiums. It appears to me to be almost more applicable to his insertions.

And so we need not trouble ourselves any more either about the insertions or about the exordiums. They both please me; the second class has pleased persons much better worth pleasing than I can

GEORGE SAINTSBURY

pretend to be; but the making or marring of the
book lies elsewhere. I do not think that it lies in
the construction, though Fielding's following of the
ancients, both sincere and satiric, has imposed a
false air of regularity upon that. The Odyssey of
Joseph, of Fanny, and of their ghostly mentor and
bodily guard is, in truth, a little haphazard, and
might have been longer or shorter without any
discreet man approving it the more or the less
therefor. The real merits lie partly in the abounding humour and satire of the artist's criticism, but
even more in the marvellous vivacity and fertility
of his creation. For the very first time in English
prose fiction every character is alive, every incident
is capable of having happened. There are lively
touches in the Elizabethan romances; but they are
buried in verbiage, swathed in stage costume, choked
and fettered by their authors' want of art. The
quality of Bunyan's knowledge of men was not
much inferior to Shakespeare's, or at least to Fielding's; but the range and the results of it were
cramped by his single theological purpose, and his
unvaried allegoric or typical form. Why Defoe did
not discover the New World of Fiction, I at least
have never been able to put into any brief critical
formula that satisfies me, and I have never seen it
put by any one else. He had not only seen it afar
off, he had made landings and descents on it; he
had carried off and exhibited in triumph natives
such as Robinson Crusoe, as Man Friday, as Moll
Flanders, as William the Quaker; but he had con-

quered, subdued, and settled no province therein.
I like *Pamela*; I like it better than some persons
who admire Richardson on the whole more than
I do seem to like it. But, as in all its author's
work, the handling seems to me academic—the
working out on paper of an ingeniously conceived
problem rather than the observation or evolution
of actual or possible life. I should not greatly fear
to push the comparison even into foreign countries;
but it is well to observe limits. Let us be content
with holding that in England at least, without
prejudice to anything further, Fielding was the
first to display the qualities of the perfect novelist
as distinguished from the romancer.

What are those qualities as shown in *Joseph
Andrews*? The faculty of arranging a probable
and interesting course of action is one, of course,
and Fielding showed it here. But I do not think
that it is at any time the greatest one; and nobody
denies that he made great advances in this direction
later. The faculty of lively dialogue is another;
and that he has not often been refused; but much
the same may be said of it. The interspersing of
appropriate description is another; but here also
we shall not find him exactly a paragon. It is in
character—the chief *differentia* of the novel as
distinguished not merely from its elder sister the
romance, and its cousin the drama, but still more
from every other kind of literature—that Fielding
stands even here pre-eminent. No one that I can
think of, except his greatest successor in the present

century, has the same unfailing gift of breathing life into every character he creates or borrows; and even Thackeray draws, if I may use the phrase, his characters more in the flat and less in the round than Fielding. Whether in Blifil he once failed, we must discuss hereafter; he has failed nowhere in *Joseph Andrews*. Some of his sketches may require the caution that they are eighteenth-century men and women; some the warning that they are obviously caricatured, or set in designed profile, or merely sketched. But they are all alive. The finical estimate of Gray (it is a horrid joy to think how perfectly capable Fielding was of having joined in that practical joke of the young gentlemen of Cambridge, which made Gray change his college), while dismissing these light things with patronage, had to admit that "parson Adams is perfectly well, so is Mrs. Slipslop." "They *were*, Mr. Gray," said some one once, "they were more perfectly well, and in a higher kind, than anything you ever did; though you were a pretty workman too."

Yes, parson Adams is perfectly well, and so is Mrs. Slipslop. But so are they all. Even the hero and heroine, tied and bound as they are by the necessity under which their maker lay of preserving Joseph's Joseph-hood, and of making Fanny the example of a franker and less interested virtue than her sister-in-law that might have been, are surprisingly human where most writers would have made them sticks. And the rest require no allowance. Lady Booby, few as are the strokes given to her, is not much less alive than Lady Bellaston. Mr. Trulliber, monster and not at all delicate monster as he is, is also a man, and when he lays it down that no one even in his own house shall drink when he "caaled vurst," one can but pay his maker the tribute of that silent shudder of admiration which hails the addition of one more everlasting entity to the world of thought and fancy. And Mr. Tow-wouse is real, and Mrs. Tow-wouse is more real still, and Betty is real; and the coachman, and Miss Grave-airs, and all the wonderful crew from first to last. The dresses they wear, the manners they exhibit, the laws they live under, the very foods and drinks they live upon, are "past like the shadows on glasses"—to the comfort and rejoicing of some, to the greater or less sorrow of others. But *they* are there—alive, full of blood, full of breath as we are, and, in truth, I fear a little more so. For some purposes a century is a gap harder to cross and more estranging than a couple of millenniums. But in their case the gap is nothing; and it is not too much to say that as they have stood the harder test, they will stand the easier. There are very striking differences between Nausicaa and Mrs. Slipslop; there are differences not less striking between Mrs. Slipslop and Beatrice. But their likeness is a stranger and more wonderful thing than any of their unlikenesses. It is that they are all women, that they are all live citizenesses of the Land of Matters Unforgot, the fashion whereof passeth not away, and the franchise whereof, once acquired, assures immortality.

ABRAHAM LINCOLN AS ORATOR AND LETTER-WRITER

By Lord Bryce

No man since Washington has become to Americans so familiar or so beloved a figure as Abraham Lincoln. He is to them the representative and typical American, the man who best embodies the political ideals of the nation. He is typical in the fact that he sprang from the masses of the people, that he remained through his whole career a man of the people, that his chief desire was to be in accord with the beliefs and wishes of the people, that he never failed to trust in the people and to rely on their support. Every native American knows his life and his speeches. His anecdotes and witticisms have passed into the thought and the conversation of the whole nation as those of no other statesman have done.

He belongs, however, not only to the United States, but to the whole of civilised mankind. It is no exaggeration to say that he has, within the last thirty years, grown to be a conspicuous figure in the history of the modern world. Without him, the course of events, not only in the Western hemisphere but in Europe also, would have been different, for he was called to guide at the greatest crisis of its fate a State already mighty, and now far more mighty than in his days, and the guidance he gave has affected the march of events ever since. A life and a character such as his ought to be known to and comprehended by Europeans as well as by Americans. Among Europeans, it is especially Englishmen who ought to appreciate him and understand the significance of his life, for he came of an English stock, he spoke the English tongue, his action told upon the progress of events and the shaping of opinion in all British communities everywhere more than it has done upon any other nation outside America itself.

Lincoln's speeches make him known by his words as readers of history know him by his deeds. In popularly-governed countries the great statesman is almost of necessity an orator, though his eminence as a speaker may be no true measure either of his momentary power or of his permanent fame, for wisdom, courage and tact bear little direct relation to the gift for speech. But whether that gift be present in greater or in lesser degree, the character and ideas of a statesman are best studied through his own words. This is particularly true of Lincoln, because he was not what may be called a professional orator. There have been famous orators whose speeches we may read for the beauty of their language or for the wealth of ideas they contain, with comparatively little regard to the circumstances of time and place that led to their being

delivered. Lincoln is not one of these. His speeches
need to be studied in close relation to the occasions
which called them forth. They are not philosophical lucubrations or brilliant displays of rhetoric.
They are a part of his life. They are the expression
of his convictions, and derive no small part of their
weight and dignity from the fact that they deal
with grave and urgent questions, and express the
spirit in which he approached those questions. Few
great characters stand out so clearly revealed by
their words, whether spoken or written, as he does.

Accordingly Lincoln's discourses are not like
those of nearly all the men whose eloquence has
won them fame. When we think of such men as
Pericles, Demosthenes, Æschines, Cicero, Horten-
sius, Burke, Sheridan, Erskine, Canning, Webster,
Gladstone, Bright, Massillon, Vergniaud, Castelar,
we think of exuberance of ideas or of phrases, of
a command of appropriate similies or metaphors, of
the gifts of invention and of exposition, of imaginative flights, or outbursts of passion fit to stir and
rouse an audience to like passion. We think of the
orator as gifted with a powerful or finely-modulated
voice, an imposing presence, a graceful delivery.
Or if—remembering that Lincoln was by profession
a lawyer and practised until he became President of
the United States—we think of the special gifts
which mark the forensic orator, we should expect
to find a man full of ingenuity and subtlety, one
dexterous in handling his case in such wise as to
please and capture the judge or the jury whom he

addresses, one skilled in those rhetorical devices and strokes of art which can be used, when need be, to engage the listener's feelings and distract his mind from the real merits of the issue.

Of all this kind of talent there was in Lincoln but little. He was not an artful pleader; indeed, it was said of him that he could argue well only those cases in the justice of which he personally believed, and was unable to make the worse appear the better reason. For most of the qualities which the world admires in Cicero or in Burke we should look in vain in Lincoln's speeches. They are not fine pieces of exquisite diction, fit to be declaimed as school exercises or set before students as models of composition.

What, then, are their merits? and why do they deserve to be valued and remembered? How comes it that a man of first-rate powers was deficient in qualities appertaining to his own profession which men less remarkable have possessed?

To answer this question, let us first ask what were the preparation and training Abraham Lincoln had for oratory, whether political or forensic.

Born in rude and abject poverty, he had never any education, except what he gave himself, till he was approaching manhood. Not even books wherewith to inform and train his mind were within his reach. No school, no university, no legal faculty had any part in training his powers. When he became a lawyer and a politician, the years most favourable to continuous study had already passed, and the opportunities he found for reading were very scanty. He knew but few authors in general literature, though he knew those few thoroughly. He taught himself a little mathematics, but he could read no language save his own, and can have had only the faintest acquaintance with European history or with any branch of philosophy.

The want of regular education was not made up for by the persons among whom his lot was cast. Till he was a grown man, he never moved in any society from which he could learn those things with which the mind of an orator or a statesman ought to be stored. Even after he had gained some legal practice, there was for many years no one for him to mix with except the petty practitioners of a petty town, men nearly all of whom knew little more than he did himself.

Schools gave him nothing, and society gave him nothing. But he had a powerful intellect and a resolute will. Isolation fostered not only self-reliance but the habit of reflection, and, indeed, of prolonged and intense reflection. He made all that he knew a part of himself. He thought everything out for himself. His convictions were his own— clear and coherent. He was not positive or opinionated, and he did not deny that at certain moments he pondered and hesitated long before he decided on his course. But though he could keep a policy in suspense, waiting for events to guide him, he did not waver. He paused and reconsidered, but it was never his way either to go back upon a decision once made, or to waste time in vain regrets that all he expected had not been attained. He took advice readily, and left many things to his ministers; but he did not lean upon his advisers. Without vanity or ostentation, he was always independent, self-contained, prepared to take full responsibility for his acts.

That he was keenly observant of all that passed under his eyes, that his mind played freely round everything it touched, we know from the accounts of his talk, which first made him famous in the town and neighbourhood where he lived. His humour, and his memory for anecdotes which he could bring out to good purpose, at the right moment, are qualities which Europe deems distinctively American, but no great man of action in the nineteenth century, even in America, possessed them in the same measure. Seldom has so acute a power of observation been found united to so abundant a power of sympathy.

These remarks may seem to belong to a study of his character rather than of his speeches, yet they are not irrelevant, because the interest of his speeches lies in their revelation of his character. Let us, however, return to his speeches and his letters, some of which are scarcely less noteworthy than are the speeches.

What are the distinctive merits of these speeches and letters? There is less humour in them than his reputation as a humorist would have led us to expect. They are serious, grave, practical. We feel that the man does not care to play over the surface of the subject, or to use it as a way of displaying his cleverness. He is trying to get right down to the very foundation of the matter and tell us what his real thoughts about it are. In this respect he sometimes reminds us of Bismarck's speeches, which, in their rude, broken, forth-darting way, always go straight to their destined aim; always hit the nail on the head. So too, in their effort to grapple with fundamental facts, Lincoln's bear a sort of likeness to Cromwell's speeches, though Cromwell has far less power of utterance, and always seems to be wrestling with the difficulty of finding language to convey to others what is plain, true and weighty to himself. This difficulty makes the great Protector, though we can usually see what he is driving at, frequently confused and obscure. Lincoln, however, is always clear. Simplicity, directness and breadth are the notes of his thought. Aptness, clearness, and again sim-plicity are the notes of his diction. The American speakers of his generation, like most of those of the preceding generation, but unlike those of that earlier generation to which Alexander Hamilton, John Adams, Marshall and Madison belonged, were generally infected by a floridity which made them a by-word in Europe. Even men of brilliant talent, such as Edward Everett, were by no means free from this straining after effect by highly-coloured phrases and theatrical effects. Such faults have to-day virtually vanished from the United

States, largely from a change in public taste, to which perhaps the example set by Lincoln himself may have contributed. In the forties and fifties florid rhetoric was rampant, especially in the West and South, where taste was less polished than in the older States. That Lincoln escaped it is a striking mark of his independence as well as of his greatness. There is no superfluous ornament in his orations, nothing tawdry, nothing otiose. For the most part, he addresses the reason of his hearers, and credits them with desiring to have none but solid arguments laid before them. When he does appeal to emotion, he does it quietly, perhaps even solemnly. The note struck is always a high note. The impressiveness of the appeal comes not from fervid vehemence of language, but from the sincerity of his own convictions. Sometimes one can see that through its whole course the argument is suffused by the speaker's feeling, and when the time comes for the feeling to be directly expressed, it glows not with fitful flashes, but with the steady heat of an intense and strenuous soul.

The impression which most of the speeches leave on the reader is that their matter has been carefully thought over even when the words have not been learnt by heart. But there is an anecdote that on one occasion, early in his career, Lincoln went to a public meeting not in the least intending to speak, but presently being called for by the audience, rose in obedience to the call, and delivered a long address so ardent and thrilling that the reporters dropped

LORD BRYCE

their pencils and, absorbed in watching him, forgot
to take down what he said. It has also been stated,
on good authority, that on his way in the railroad
cars to the dedication of the monument on the
field of Gettysburg, he turned to a Pennsylvanian
gentleman who was sitting beside him and remarked,
" I suppose I shall be expected to say something
this afternoon; lend me a pencil and a bit of
paper," and that he thereupon jotted down the
notes of a speech which has become the best known
and best remembered of all his utterances, so that
some of its words and sentences have passed into
the minds of all educated men everywhere.

That famous Gettysburg speech is the best
example one could desire of the characteristic
quality of Lincoln's eloquence. It is a short speech.
It is wonderfully terse in expression. It is quiet,
so quiet that at the moment it did not make upon
the audience, an audience wrought up by a long
and highly-decorated harangue from one of the
prominent orators of the day, an impression at all
commensurate to that which it began to make as
soon as it was read over America and Europe.
There is in it not a touch of what we call rhetoric,
or of any striving after effect. Alike in thought
and in language it is simple, plain, direct. But it
states certain truths and principles in phrases so
aptly chosen and so forcible, that one feels as if
those truths could have been conveyed in no other
words, and as if this deliverance of them were made
for all time. Words so simple and so strong could

72

have come only from one who had meditated so long upon the primal facts of American history and popular government that the truths those facts taught him had become like the truths of mathematics in their clearness, their breadth, and their precision.

The speeches on Slavery read strange to us now, when slavery as a living system has been dead for forty years, dead and buried hell deep under the detestation of mankind. It is hard for those whose memory does not go back to 1865 to realise that down till then it was not only a terrible fact, but was defended—defended by many otherwise good men, defended not only by pseudo-scientific anthropologists as being in the order of nature, but by ministers of the Gospel, out of the sacred Scriptures, as part of the ordinances of God. Lincoln's position, the position of one who had to induce slave-owning fellow-citizens to listen to him and admit persuasion into their heated and prejudiced minds, did not allow him to denounce it with horror, as we can all so easily do to-day. But though his language is calm and restrained, he never condescends to palter with slavery. He shows its innate evils and dangers with unanswerable force. The speech on the Dred Scott decision is a lucid, close and cogent piece of reasoning which, in its wide view of Constitutional issues, sometimes reminds one of Webster, sometimes even of Burke, though it does not equal the former in weight nor the latter in splendour of diction.

73

LORD BRYCE

Among the letters, perhaps the most impressive is that written to Mrs. Bixley, the mother of five sons who had died fighting for the Union in the armies of the North. It is short, and it deals with a theme on which hundreds of letters are written daily. But I do not know where the nobility of self-sacrifice for a great cause, and of the consolation which the thought of a sacrifice so made should bring, is set forth with such simple and pathetic beauty. Deep must be the fountains from which there issues so pure a stream.

The career of Lincoln is often held up to ambitious young Americans as an example to show what a man may achieve by his native strength, with no advantages of birth or environment or education. In this there is nothing improper, nothing fanciful. The moral is one which may well be drawn, and in which those on whose early life Fortune has not smiled may find encouragement. But the example is, after all, no great encouragement to ordinary men, for Lincoln was an extraordinary man.

He triumphed over the adverse conditions of his early years because Nature had bestowed on him high and rare powers. Superficial observers who saw his homely aspect and plain manners, and noted that his fellow-townsmen, when asked why they so trusted him, answered that it was for his common-sense, failed to see that his common-sense was a part of his genius. What is common-sense but the power of seeing the fundamentals of any practical question, and of disengaging them from the acci-

74

dental and transient features that may overlie these fundamentals—the power, to use a familiar expression, of getting down to bed rock? One part of this power is the faculty for perceiving what the average man will think and can be induced to do This is what keeps the superior mind in touch with the ordinary mind, and this is perhaps why the name of " common-sense " is used, because the superior mind seems in its power of comprehending others to be itself a part of the general sense of the community. All men of high practical capacity have this power. It is the first condition of success. But in men who have received a philosophical or literary education there is a tendency to embellish, for purposes of persuasion, or perhaps for their own gratification, the language in which they recommend their conclusions, or to state those conclusions in the light of large general principles, a tendency which may, unless carefully watched, carry them too high above the heads of the crowd. Lincoln, never having had such an education, spoke to the people as one of themselves. He seemed to be saying not only what each felt, but expressing the feeling just as each would have expressed it. In reality, he was quite as much above his neighbours in insight as was the polished orator or writer, but the plain directness of his language seemed to keep him on their level. His strength lay less in the form and vesture of the thought than in the thought itself, in the large, simple, practical view which he took of the position. And thus, to repeat what has been said already, the sterling merit of these speeches of his, that which made them effective when they were delivered and makes them worth reading to-day, is to be found in the justness of his conclusions and their fitness to the circumstances of the time. When he rose into higher air, when his words were clothed with stateliness and solemnity, it was the force of his conviction and the emotion that thrilled through his utterance, that printed the words deep upon the minds and drove them home to the hearts of the people.

What is a great man? Common speech, which after all must be our guide to the sense of the terms which the world uses, gives this name to many sorts of men. How far greatness lies in the power and range of the intellect, how far in the strength of the will, how far in elevation of view and aim and purpose—this is a question too large to be debated here. But of Abraham Lincoln it may be truly said that in his greatness all three elements were present. He had not the brilliance, either in thought or word or act, that dazzles, nor the restless activity that occasionally pushes to the front even persons with gifts not of the first order. He was a patient, thoughtful, melancholy man, whose intelligence, working sometimes slowly but always steadily and surely, was capacious enough to embrace, and vigorous enough to master, the incomparably difficult facts and problems he was called to deal with. His executive talent showed itself not in sudden and startling strokes, but in the calm serenity with which he formed his judgments and laid his plans, in the undismayed firmness with which he adhered to them in the face of popular clamour, of conflicting counsels from his advisers, sometimes, even, of what others deemed all but hopeless failure. These were the qualities needed in one who had to pilot the Republic through the heaviest storm that had ever broken upon it. But the mainspring of his power, and the truest evidence of his greatness, lay in the nobility of his aims, in the fervour of his conviction, in the stainless rectitude which guided his action and won for him the confidence of the people. Without these things neither the vigour of his intellect nor the firmness of his will would have availed.

There is a vulgar saying that all great men are unscrupulous. Of him it may rather be said that the note of greatness we feel in his thinking and his speech and his conduct had its source in the loftiness and purity of his character. Lincoln's is one of the careers that refute this imputation on human nature.

A POINT OF BIOGRAPHY

By Alice Meynell

There is hardly a writer now—of the third class probably not one—who has not something sharp and sad to say about the cruelty of Nature; not one who is able to attempt May in the woods without a modern reference to the manifold death and destruction with which the air, the branches, the mosses are said to be full.

But no one has paused in the course of these phrases to take notice of the curious and conspicuous fact of the suppression of death and of the dead throughout this landscape of manifest life. Where are they—all the dying, all the dead, of the populous woods? Where do they hide their little last hours, where are they buried? Where is the violence concealed? Under what gay custom and decent habit? You may see, it is true, an earthworm in a robin's beak, and may hear a thrush breaking a snail's shell; but these little things are, as it were, passed by with a kind of twinkle for apology, as by a well-bred man who does openly some little solecism which is too slight for direct mention, and which a meaner man might hide or avoid. Unless you are very modern indeed, you twinkle back at the bird.

But otherwise there is nothing visible of the havoc and the prey and plunder. It is certain that much of the visible life passes violently into other forms, flashes without pause into another flame; but not all. Amid all the killing there must be much dying. There are, for instance, few birds of prey left in our more accessible counties now, and many thousands of birds must die uncaught by a hawk and unpierced. But if their killing is done so modestly, so then is their dying also. Short lives have all these wild things, but there are innumerable flocks of them always alive; they must die, then, in innumerable flocks. And yet they keep the millions of the dead out of sight.

Now and then, indeed, they may be betrayed. It happened in a cold winter. The late frosts were so sudden, and the famine was so complete, that the birds were taken unawares. The sky and the earth conspired that February to make known all the secrets; everything was published. Death was manifest. Editors, when a great man dies, are not more resolute than was the frost of '95.

The birds were obliged to die in public. They were surprised and forced to do thus. They became like Shelley in the monument which the art and imagination of England combined to raise to his memory at Oxford.

Frost was surely at work in both cases, and in both it wrought wrong. There is a similarity of unreason in betraying the death of a bird and in exhibiting the death of Shelley. The death of a soldier—*passe encore*. But the death of Shelley was not his goal. And the death of the birds is so little characteristic of them that, as has just been said, no one in the world is aware of their dying, except only in the case of birds in cages, who, again, are compelled to die with observation. The woodland is guarded and kept by a rule. There is no display of the battlefield in the fields. There is no tale of the game-bag, no boast. The hunting goes on, but with strange decorum. You may pass a fine season under the trees, and see nothing dead except here and there where a boy has been by, or a man with a trap, or a man with a gun. There is nothing like a butcher's shop in the woods.

But the biographers have always had other ways than those of the wild world. They will not have a man to die out of sight. I have turned over scores of " Lives," not to read them, but to see whether now and again there might be a " Life " which was not more emphatically a death. But there never is a modern biography that has taken the hint of Nature. One and all, these books have the disproportionate illness, the death out of all scale.

Even more wanton than the disclosure of a death is that of a mortal illness. If the man had recovered, his illness would have been rightly his own secret. But because he did not recover, it is assumed to be news for the first comer. Which of us would suffer the details of any physical suffering, over and done in our own lives, to be displayed and described? This is not a confidence we have a mind to make; and no one is authorised to ask for attention or pity on our behalf. The story of pain ought not to be told of us, seeing that by us it would assuredly not be told.

There is only one other thing that concerns a man still more exclusively, and that is his own mental illness, or the dreams and illusions of a long delirium. When he is in common language not himself, amends should be made for so bitter a paradox; he should be allowed such solitude as is possible to the alienated spirit; he should be left to the " not himself," and spared the intrusion against which he can so ill guard that he could hardly have even resented it.

The double helplessness of delusion and death should keep the door of Rossetti's house, for example, and refuse him to the reader. His mortal illness had nothing to do with his poetry. Some rather affected objection is taken every now and then to the publication of some facts (others being already well known) in the life of Shelley. Nevertheless, these are all, properly speaking, biography. What is not biography is the detail of the accident of the manner of his death, the detail of his cremation. Or if it was to be told—told briefly—it was certainly not for marble. Shelley's death had no significance, except inasmuch as he died young. It was a detachable and disconnected incident. Ah, that was a frost of fancy and of the heart that used it so, dealing with an insignificant fact, and conferring a futile immortality. Those are ill-named biographers who seem to think that a betrayal of the ways of death is a part of their ordinary duty, and that if material enough for a last chapter does not lie to their hand they are to search it out. They, of all survivors, are called upon, in honour and reason, to look upon a death with more composure. To those who loved the dead closely, this is, for a time, impossible. To them death becomes, for a year, disproportionate. Their dreams are fixed upon it night by night. They have, in those dreams, to find the dead in some labyrinth; they have to mourn his dying and to welcome his recovery in such a mingling of distress and of always incredulous happiness as is not known even to dreams save in that first year of separation. But they are not biographers.

If death is the privacy of the woods, it is the more conspicuously secret because it is their only privacy. You may watch or may surprise everything else. The nest is retired, not hidden. The chase goes on everywhere. It is wonderful how the perpetual chase seems to cause no perpetual fear. The songs are all audible. Life is undefended, careless, nimble and noisy.

It is a happy thing that minor artists have ceased, or almost ceased, to paint dead birds. Time was when they did it continually in that British School of water-colour art, stippled, of which surrounding nations, it was agreed, were envious. They must have killed their bird to paint him, for he is not to be caught dead. A bird is more easily caught alive than dead.

A poet, on the contrary, is easily—too easily—caught dead. Minor artists now seldom stipple the bird on its back, but a good sculptor and a University together modelled their Shelley on his back, unessentially drowned; and everybody may read about the sick mind of Dante Rossetti.

GENIUS LOCI

By Vernon Lee

It had rained heavily, that last day at Verona, and
cleared up in the afternoon. I bought a bunch of
lavender for remembrance; and had some coffee,
before starting, in Piazza dei Signori. The stones
were still wet, but the sky clear. Moist clouds
were sailing above the towers; the town pigeons
pecking on the pavement and flying into the palace
crannies; swallows screaming; the sun, invisible
behind roofs, was setting. 'Tis at this hour, to the
sound of bells, that the genius of old cities seems to
gather himself up and overcome one's heart.

To certain among us, undeniably, places, localities
(I can find no reverent and tender enough expression for them in our practical, personal language)
become objects of intense and most intimate feeling.
Quite irrespective of their inhabitants, and virtually
of their written history, they can touch us like
living creatures; and one can have with them
friendship of the deepest and most satisfying sort.

To say this may seem nonsense if we think of
friendship as what it largely is, a mere practical and
in the main accidental relation, wherein exchange
of ideas and good offices, fetching and carrying for

one another, and toiling and moiling in company, plays the principal part. But there are other possibilities, surely, in friendship, its very best portion; and such may exist in our relations with places. Indeed, when I try to define the greatest good which human creatures can do us, good far transcending any practical help or intellectual guidance, it seems to express itself quite naturally in vague metaphors borrowed from those other friends who are not human beings: for it is the good of charming us, of raising our spirits, of subduing our feelings into serenity and happiness; of singing in our memory like melodies; and bringing out, even as melodies do when we hear or remember them, whatever small twitter of music there may be in our soul. These are the highest gifts of our human affections; and surely we receive them equally, nay, sometimes even better, from the impersonal reality whom I call, for want of a better name, and from a lurking wish to bring some thanksgiving, the Genius Loci.

Genius Loci. A divinity, certainly, great or small as the case may be, and deserving of some silent worship. But, for mercy's sake, not a personification; not a man or woman with mural crown and attributes, and detestable definite history, like the dreadful ladies who sit round the Place de la Concorde. To think of a place or a country in human shape is, for all the practice of rhetoricians, not to think of it at all. No, no. The Genius Loci, like all worthy divinities, is of the substance

85

of our heart and mind, a spiritual reality. And as for visible embodiment, why that is the place itself, or the country; and the features and speech are the lie of the land, pitch of the streets, sound of bells or of weirs; above all, perhaps, that strangely impressive combination, noted by Virgil, of " rivers washing round old city walls ":

Fluminaque antiquos subterlabentia muros.

That line of Virgil, in a passage which, like so many of Dante's, shows the deep power of localities over the Latin mind, must naturally suggest the Adige; and bring me back to those solitary days at Verona, when I found myself returning continually to watch the great reddish swirls of the river, with the big floating mills rocked on their surface. And this reminds me that, although what I call the Genius Loci can never be personified, we may yet feel him nearer and more potent in some individual monument or feature of the landscape. He is immanent very often, and subduing our hearts most deeply, at a given turn of a road; or a path cut in terraces in a hillside, with view of great distant mountains; or, again, in a church like Classe, near Ravenna; most of all, perhaps, in the meeting-place of streams, or the mouth of a river, both of which draw our feet and thoughts time after time, we know not why or wherefore. The genius of places lurks there; or, more strictly, *he is it*.

I have compared the feelings we can have for places with the feelings awakened in us by certain of our friends—feelings of love and gratitude, but not of prosaic familiarity or wish for community of commonplace. But as there are, or at least may be, some human relationships which constitute the bulk of life, and yet remain its poetry, so there are one or two places for every individual, where he may live habitually, yet never lose the sense of delight, wonder, and gratitude. Certain river districts, no doubt, in England; and, for the present writer, the Tuscan valleys and stony hillsides.

The type of all such places is, however, Rome. Its legendary power over our heart cannot be fathomed even by those of its most devoted lovers, who have known it only for its own sake, and on purpose to enjoy, as a holiday, its Genius Loci. It takes months and years of prosaic residence to really appreciate the extraordinary fashion in which the troubles and trivialities of life, so far from diminishing this imaginative power, are subdued into proper insignificance; lost in Rome's seriousness and serenity, and in that assurance which Rome tacitly gives, like some rare human beings, that life, though short, is worthy of being lived with earnestness and grace.

But it was not of such an exceptional, nay unique, case that I was thinking when I entered on the subject of our friendship with places; not of the love unflagging and for ever, but rather of mere *amours de voyage* (in the most worthy sense) where, though the remembrance may be long, the actual moment of meeting (" now we have met we are safe," as Whitman says) is necessarily very brief.

Trifling incidents, standing in these matters like a book read together or a flower given in more human relationships, sometimes have the effect of turning a locality from a geographical expression into something of one's very own; indeed, one charm of fishing or shooting, for meditative persons, is undoubtedly that it brings a more intimate connection between places and oneself. In the same manner I have a feeling as of something like a troth plighted, or a religious rite accomplished, binding the place and me together, from having drunk once from a spring which spirted across the remote, "back of beyond" road between Subiaco and Tivoli, one March day that the dust was rising in whirlpools. Nay, I feel sometimes as if I should like not to drink, but to pour a libation or hang up a garland in honour of the Genius Loci, indeed. . . .

But enough. I suppose it was some silly sentiment of this kind which, when I had been three or four times to look at the floating mills of the Adige, made me buy that bunch of lavender in the marketplace of Verona, when the sun was setting, and the swallows whirring, and the bells beginning to ring the presence of the divinity of places.

SIR THOMAS BROWNE

By JOHN ADDINGTON SYMONDS

THE reputation of Sir Thomas Browne is founded on his *Religio Medici* and *Enquiry into Vulgar Errors*, and also on some tracts, the most remarkable of which are entitled *Hydriotaphia* or *Urn Burial* and *The Garden of Cyrus*. If nothing but his *Vulgar Errors* had been handed down to us, we might have numbered him among the possessors of vast and recondite learning, who wasted ingenuity and patience upon subjects of little interest and of no permanent value. This work of erudition does not display the author's charm as a thinker and a stylist; his unique mental and moral qualities are not so clearly reflected in it as those of Burton, for example, in the *Anatomy of Melancholy*. But the case is different with Browne's other compositions. The higher gifts of style which he commands, the majesty and harmony of his language, the nobility of his sentiments, the depth and range of his imagination, and the far-stretched grandeur of his speculative fancy, are so brilliantly exhibited throughout the *Religio Medici*, in one or two sonorous passages of *Cyrus's Garden*, and in the peroration of the treatise on *Urn Burial*, that we must place him among the foremost writers of English prose. It is as a great master of diction, as a rhetorician in the highest sense of that abused word, as one who improvised solemn cathedral voluntaries upon the organ of our language in its period of cumbrous and scholastic pomp, that Sir Thomas Browne proclaims himself the rival of Jeremy Taylor and the peer of Milton in their highest flights of cadenced prose. Like all English prosaists before the time of Dryden, he is unequal in literary manner, composing apparently without a fixed idea of style, indulging in whims and oddities, attaining his most sublime effects by felicities of verbal music rather than by conscious mastery of art. " He fell into an age," says Johnson, " in which our language began to lose the stability which it obtained in the time of Elizabeth; and was considered by every writer as a subject on which he might try his plastic skill, by moulding it according to his own fancy. Milton, in consequence of this encroaching licence, began to introduce the Latin idiom: and Browne, though he gave less disturbance to our structures and phraseology, yet poured in a multitude of exotic words. His style is, indeed, a tissue of many languages; a mixture of heterogeneous words, brought together from distant regions, with terms originally appropriated to one art, and drawn by violence into the service of another." In the main, this criticism is just. What Coleridge called Browne's " hyperlatinism," renders his prose no model for the student. Its defects are obvious and patent. Its excellences are such as only the greatest artist in language, imbued with profound thought, and inspired with glowing imagination, can hope to emulate. Yet before the close of this Introduction, I think it will be clear that Sir Thomas Browne, in his best moments, produced not only sentences, but lengthy passages of flawless quality—inimitable periods governed by unerring rhythm in which various elements of speech are harmonised by the controlling sense of assonantal and alliterative music.

Sir Thomas Browne was born in London on the 19th of October, 1605. He died at Norwich on the 19th of October, 1682, having exactly reached the age of seventy-seven—a circumstance which, could he have transmitted posthumous reflections on his own death, would doubtless have inspired his curious mind with many mystic contemplations. His father was a merchant, born of a good Cheshire stock, who had acquired considerable wealth. In temperament this man, of whom we know almost nothing, may have resembled his more illustrious son; for it is recorded of the boy's infancy that " his father used to open his breast when he was asleep, and kiss it in prayers over him, as 'tis said of Origen's father, that the Holy Ghost would take possession there." These are the words of Sir Thomas's daughter, Mrs. Lyttleton, who probably had them from his own lips. A certain air of mystery and consecration, as of one dedicated, for whom nothing could be common or unclean, to whom his own life seemed " a miracle of thirty years," and the visible world "an hieroglyphical and shadowed lesson " of the thoughts of God, surrounded the man from childhood to old age.

He had the misfortune to lose his father early. His mother shortly afterwards married Sir Thomas Dutton, who proved, it is asserted, a rapacious guardian. The boy was sent to Winchester, and in 1623 proceeded to Pembroke College, Oxford, where he took his B.A. degree in 1627. His share of the paternal estate amounted to some £6000, and this was a fair fortune at that period. The natural bent of his genius toward physical science determined his choice of medicine as a profession. After practising a short while in Oxfordshire, he travelled through Ireland with his stepfather, and then set out upon a tour in Europe. At Montpellier and Padua he prosecuted medical studies, and acquired the French and Italian languages. Returning northward, he obtained a degree of M.D. at Leyden in 1633. When he reached England, he settled for some time as practising physician at Shipley Hall, near Halifax; and it was probably during that residence that he composed the *Religio Medici*. Friends induced him to leave a retreat where his talents had too little opportunity for their display. Accordingly, upon the joint solicitations of Sir Nicholas Bacon, Sir Charles Le Gros, and Drs. Lushington and Lewyn—all of them important Norfolk worthies—he established himself in the old city of Norwich, where the

remainder of his life was spent. This took place
in 1637, when he had reached the age of thirty-two,
and had still forty-five years to live.

We do not know precisely when the *Religio
Medici* was completed; but the commonly received
date of 1635 is probably correct. Sir Thomas
Browne asserts that he composed the treatise for
his "private exercise and satisfaction," not intending it for publication. As the fashion then was,
he submitted his work in MS. to a friend. "Being
communicated to one, it became common unto
many, and was by transcription successively cor-
rupted, until it arrived in a most depraved copy at
the press." There is no reason to doubt this statement. The book itself bears indisputable marks
of having been the unpremeditated and garrulous
outpouring of "leisurable hours." Its charm
consists in a certain *naïveté* of self-revelation, a
genial and inoffensive egotism, indulging itself in
reveries and speculations, which shall perhaps be
overheard by a kindly reader, but are not meant
for the great public. The method of *Pseudodoxia*,
designed for publication by its author, is quite
different and far less fascinating. Numerous MS.
copies, still in existence, confirm the truth of Sir
Thomas's account; and the first edition of *Religio
Medici*, which appeared in 1642, was therefore
certainly surreptitious. It immediately attracted
attention. Lord Dorset sent the little volume
to Sir Kenelm Digby, then under arrest in
Winchester House, who eagerly perused it and

straightway penned his Observations or Animad-
versions upon its speculative contents. This critique
also circulated in MS.; whereupon Dr. Browne
wrote courteously to the author, pointing out that
the *Religio Medici* of 1642 was "broken and
imperfect," altered in many senses by addition,
omission, and transposition, "without his assent
or privacy," and begging Digby to delay the publication of his remarks until he could present the
world with a correct copy of his book. The authorised edition appeared in 1643, together with Sir
Kenelm Digby's observations. This correspondence,
no doubt, gave the work some public fame. Its
intrinsic merits soon secured for it European
celebrity. It was translated into Latin, Dutch,
French, German, and perhaps also Italian. It
had the honour of being placed upon the Index
Expurgatorius of the Roman Church, where it is
still quoted. Dr. Johnson ascribes its success to
" the novelty of paradoxes, the dignity of sentiment,
the quick succession of images, the multitude of
abstruse allusions, the subtlety of disquisition, and
the strength of language." But it also obtained
what the French call a *succès de scandale*. Strangely
enough, its theological opinions then passed for
over-bold in the direction of free-thought. Dr.
Browne had set himself to depict the creed of a
man dedicated to scientific studies, versed in analysis,
trained to sceptical inquiry, the member of a profession vulgarly credited with irreligion. He showed
that his own mind was open upon many points,

SIR THOMAS BROWNE

and that he had not abstained from serious delvings round about the roots of faith. But instead of tending toward the atheism of which he was by some accused, he maintained that an atheist could not exist. His own belief in Christianity was so impassioned that he longed for greater difficulties than those offered by the creeds. He refused to accept the Copernican hypothesis, because it seemed to contradict scripture. He proved himself to be a " God-intoxicated man," penetrated through and through with the sense of the divine in nature. He declared himself, moreover, a Christian of the Anglican type, devoted to the Church of England; heterodox only in the tolerance he professed for the Roman Catholic ritual, and the yearning sympathy he felt for those whose faith savoured of larger credulity and more bounteous superstition. The personal nature of his piety, however, a piety which seemed to be the exhalation of his own peculiar temperament, together with a certain self-complacent parade of curious opinions as though they savoured of the sceptical spirit, may have offended contemporaries who demanded more rigid utterances of orthodoxy.

In the *Religio Medici* Dr. Browne had spoken with lordly contempt of matrimony. He expressed his regret that the human race could not be propagated like trees, instead of by the " vulgar and trivial way " of marriage. He also maintained that " the whole world was made for man, but only the twelfth part of man for woman," she being

" the rib or crooked part of man." That he should
have taken to himself a wife just before the divul-
gation of these propositions, was a practical paradox
which exposed him to some sarcasm. The lady
on whom his choice fell, and to whom he was
united in 1641, lived with him through forty-one
years of happy wedlock, bore him eleven children,
and survived his decease two years, retaining
deep veneration for his memory. She was Dorothy,
daughter of Edward Mileham, Esq., of a substantial
Norfolk family. Two of their sons and two of their
daughters may here be mentioned. Edward Browne
inherited his father's scientific interests, followed
his profession, and rose to eminence as a London
physician. Thomas, a youth of rare spirit and
ability, died after a short but brilliant career in the
English naval service. Anne married a grandson
of Lord Fairfax; and Elizabeth, to whom we owe
a few precious records of her father, became the
wife of Major George Lyttleton. The domestic
correspondence of this family, a large portion of
which has been published, reveals very agreeable
relations between parents and children. The letters
of the sons upon their foreign travels are particularly
interesting. Sir Thomas Browne's replies breathe
a spirit of large wisdom, fatherly affection, and
liberal knowledge of the world, which proves him
to have been far other than the " absent and solitary
man " some critics have depicted. The speculative
philosopher and consummate artist, with whom
we are acquainted through his writings, co-existed

with a shrewd physician and a prudent master of his household in Sir Thomas Browne.

After the date of his marriage, Browne's life pursued its even and uneventful tenor at Norwich. He attained considerable fame and acquired some wealth in his profession. All the time which he could spare from business was devoted to study. He brought together a large library, and amassed huge stores of learning in antiquities, languages, and the curiosities of erudition. Yet he was no bookworm. Among the collections found after his death and posthumously published, we discover notes upon the monuments and ancient buildings of Norwich, exhaustive treatises on the birds and fishes of Norfolk, speculations supported by practical experiments upon the process of congelation and the nature of bubbles, dissertations upon the plants of the Bible, and miscellaneous tracts, which prove that he diligently pursued the inductive method of inquiry into nature. He was avowedly the first to notice and analyse the substance called adipocene, which results from certain forms of putrefaction in the grave. He showed rare sagacity in indicating the future imperial greatness of America. He corresponded with the best men of his time, Evelyn and Dugdale being obliged to him for knowledge communicated on their several subjects. Of his home at Norwich, Evelyn has bequeathed this pleasant glimpse: " His whole house and garden being a paradise and cabinet of rarities, and that of the best collections, especially medals, books,

plants, and natural things." It only remains to be
mentioned that Charles II. conferred on him the
honour of knighthood in 1671. This may have
been gratifying to the old man, although he made
no mention of it; for Sir Thomas Browne, throughout and after the troubles of the Great Rebellion,
remained a staunch Royalist and Church of England
man. The execution of the King he called "The
horrid murther of King Charles I."

Browne's quiet and studious life continued
through the Civil Wars and Commonwealth, only
diversified by the publication of his successive
volumes. Their dates are interesting. That of
Religio Medici, 1643, is the year of Chalgrove
Field, the year of the Solemn League and Covenant.
The *Enquiry into Vulgar Errors* saw the light in
1646, the year of King Charles's retreat to Newcastle. *Hydriotaphia* and *The Garden of Cyrus* were
published together in 1658, the year of Cromwell's
death. Yet no syllable in any of these writings,
notwithstanding their profound and penetrative
meditations upon vicissitudes in human lives and
empires, betrays the author's partisanship in the
tragedy enacted on the world's great stage around
him. His thoughts on those subjects quietly rested,
like the bones discovered by him at Great Wal-
singham, "under the drums and tramplings of three
conquests." This is the proper attitude of one not
called by station to control the body politic, but
destined by genius to the humbler function of
securing an immortality of literary fame.

Pseudodoxia Epidemica, elsewise entitled *Enquiries into Vulgar and Common Errors,* might be named the sweepings of its author's note-books. So far as its plan is concerned, the publication could have been indefinitely postponed; and various collections brought to sight after his death, show that Sir Thomas Browne was occupied with the same class of problems during a life-time. Probably he felt that he had done enough to cast the light of sense and judgment upon the lurking holes of popular credulity. I think, too, that the part of the work which occupied his mind most was the philosophical introduction. This is an essay on the sources of false opinion, which is not unworthy to be ranked with Bacon's famous Analysis of Idols. He traces the causes of common errors to the infirmity of human nature, which made Adam ignorantly fall in Eden; to the erroneous disposition of the people, who in all their judgments are weak, illiterate, and greedy of fables; to logical fallacies and misleading subtleties of etymology; to taking things on trust and mental indolence, defined by him as supinity; to blind adoration of antiquity and authority; and lastly, as though to sum up the whole matter in a general indictment, to the ever-restless malevolence of Satan. This survey of the founts of human credulousness may be reckoned more than psychologically exhaustive. In the superfluous speculations upon man's antediluvian nature, and in the wide sphere allotted to the devil as an active agent in human affairs,

Browne's peculiar limitations appear. They were limitations not extraordinary in his age, but somewhat singularly combined in him with philosophical acumen, indicating his real magnitude as a rhetorician rather than as the pioneer of modern thought. We comprehend from these first principles of his how it was that the learned author of a treatise upon Vulgar Errors believed in witchcraft, and gave evidence at Norwich which helped to convict two miserable victims of vulgar superstition.

Pseudodoxia is not a book to read through now. We may turn its pages over for our recreation. We can dip into it profitably here and there. It will amuse us to study the old lore of griffins and mandrakes, mistletoe and laurel, the phœnix and the salamander. We shall be interested to find why Jews do not stink, and what is the superstition of saluting after sneezing, wherefore negroes are black, what was then thought about gipsies, and how absurd it seemed to paint Adam and Eve in Paradise with navels. In a word, the book deals with the obsolete curiosities of an antiquated cabinet. Scarcely more than two centuries divide us from the time when those problems seemed to be of actual importance, and when those superstitions had to be dispelled by argument. It would be uncritical to regard Browne as a literary Don Quixote, tilting against windmills. Yet his collections have hardly more value at the present moment than the stuffed animals and paltry fossils upon which our vast scientific museums have been built up. There is no method, no firm grip upon the world, in that erudition smelling of dust and mould. And, what is more to the purpose of this essay, Sir Thomas Browne has not displayed his great qualities as a writer in the redaction of his treatise. The poet, the rhetorician, the wizard of sonorous and melodiously cadenced English, makes himself rarely felt in the *Enquiry into Vulgar Errors*.

Hydriotaphia is a work which calls for no explanatory comment. The design is simple, the intention plain, the erudition singular, the language sustained on a majestic note of eloquence. Yet I cannot omit the occasion which the mention of it offers, for pointing out the rarer qualities of Sir Thomas Browne's style, here displayed in rich maturity and heavy-scented blossom. The opening phrase of his dedication to Sir Thomas Le Gros —" When the funeral pyre was out, and the last valediction over, men took a lasting adieu of their interred friends, little expecting the curiosity of future ages should comment upon their ashes ": —this phrase strikes a key-note to the sombre harmonies which follow, connecting the ossuaries of the dead, the tears quenched in the dust of countless generations, with the vivid sympathy and scrutinising sagacity of the living writer. It is not my part to epitomise the substance of this essay. I will only call attention to the unique feeling for verbal tone, for what may be called the musical colour of words, for crumbling cadences and the reverberation of stationary sounds in

cavernous recesses, which is discernible at large
throughout the dissertation. How simple, for
example, seems the collocation of vocables in this
phrase—" Under the drums and tramplings of
three conquests "! And yet with what impeccable
instinct the vowels are arranged; how naturally,
how artfully, the rhythm falls! Take another,
and, this time, a complete sentence—" But the
iniquity of oblivion blindly scattereth her poppy,
and deals with the memory of men without distinction to merit of perpetuity." Take yet another
—" The brother of death daily haunts us with
dying mementoes." And another—" But man is
a noble animal, splendid in ashes, and pompous
in the grave, solemnising nativities and deaths with
equal lustre, nor omitting ceremonies of bravery
in the infamy of his nature." Such sentences,
the common warp and woof of *Urn Burial*, match
with their numerous prose the lofty rime which
Milton built in blank verse periods of *Paradise
Lost* and *Paradise Regained*.

Some remarks, of a different import, must be
devoted to *The Garden of Cyrus*; since space will
not permit me to include this treatise in the present
volume. In effect it is a dissertation on the Quincunx; that figure familiar to all of us in the five
of a die or a domino, and in which, when oftentimes repeated, trees have from old time been
planted. Sir Thomas Browne discourses at large
upon the gardens of antiquity, and having mentioned Cyrus, who first used the quincunx in his

Persian groves, passes by degrees to the consideration of "every production of art and nature, in which he could find any decussation or approaches to the form of a quincunx." Together with much that is merely whimsical, the treatise abounds in curious and exact observations upon a great variety of plants, evincing its author's minute acquaintance with their habits and his practical researches in vegetable physiology. His tendency toward a species of Pythagorean mysticism is manifested by the enthusiasm with which he hunts the number five, and traces quinary arrangement in all the subtleties of nature and the ingenuities of human skill. For his intelligence, as Coleridge has remarked, there are "quincunxes in heaven above, quincunxes in earth below, quincunxes in the mind of man, quincunxes in tones, in optic nerves, in roots of trees, in leaves, in every thing." That aura, or spiritual afflatus of divine mystery, which permeated his imagination, tempted him to follow such lines of inquiry. He thought that, when supported by rational experiment and observation, they might lead to luciferous discoveries. For whoso works upon these hints "shall not," he says, "pass his hours in vulgar speculations. He shall not fall on trite or trivial disquisitions." To avoid "*crambe* verities and questions over-queried" was ever a main object with this fastidious student. Yet he did not suffer himself to be the victim of his own conceits. A vein of humour, a subrisive irony runs through his more fantastic meditations on the

quincunx; and at the end of the essay, he dismisses
the main subject in a passage of such harmonious
eloquence and such fine fancy, as leaves the reader
with the sound of music and the stirring of cool
night airs to soothe his puzzled brain. It appears
that Sir Thomas had been writing late into the
night in his study at Norwich. Declining con-
stellations warned him to lay his pen down and to
yield to sleep. This peroration is characteristic
of his somewhat desultory manner; the manner
of one discoursing music to himself, and delighting
in the devious melodies of improvisation, without
external stimulus, without the regard of any audience
but his own vigilant thoughts:

But the quincunx[1] of heaven runs low, and 'tis
time to close the first parts of knowledge. We are
unwilling to spin out our awaking thoughts into
the phantasms of sleep, which often continueth pre-
cogitations, making cables of cobwebs, and wilder-
nesses of handsome groves. Beside, Hippocrates[2]
hath spoke so little, and the oneirocritical[3]
masters
have left such frigid interpretations from plants,
that there is little encouragement to dream of Paradise itself. Nor will the sweetest delight of gardens
afford much comfort in sleep: wherein the dulness
of that sense shakes hands with delectable odours;
and though in the bed of Cleopatra,[4] can hardly
with any delight raise up the ghost of a rose.
Night, which Pagan theology could make the
daughter of Chaos, affords no advantage to the
description of order; although no lower than that

[1] The constellation of the Hyades.
[2] *De Insomniis.*
[3] *Artemidorus et Apomazar.*
[4] Strewed with roses.

mass can we derive its genealogy. All things began in order, so shall they end, and so shall they begin again; according to the ordainer of order and mystical mathematicks of the city of heaven.

Though Somnus in Homer be sent to rouse up Agamemnon, I find no such effects in these drowsy approaches of sleep. To keep our eyes open longer, were but to act our Antipodes. The huntsmen are up in America, and they are already past their first sleep in Persia. But who can be drowsy at that hour which freed us from everlasting sleep? or have slumbering thoughts at that time, when sleep itself must end, and, as some conjecture, all shall awake again?

"Think you," wrote Coleridge on the margin opposite this passage, "that there was ever such a reason given before for going to bed at midnight; to wit, that if we did not, we should be *acting the part of our Antipodes?* And then: *The huntsmen are up in America!* What life, what fancy! Does the whimsical knight give us, thus, the essence of gunpowder tea, and call it an opiate?" Words could hardly be found better suited to describe the thrill of pleasure aroused in epicures of style, by the sudden sallies and unexpected epigrams of fancy, which alternate with massive rhetorical pageantry in Sir Thomas Browne's prose.

Of his three posthumously published pieces, one is a short unfinished tract on Dreams, a topic which had singular attraction for its author, and which he splendidly illustrated in the second part of *Religio Medici*. The second is a letter written to a friend upon the decease of a young man, whom Browne had attended during his last illness.

It has a value beyond that of most consolatory epistles; for it conveys a solemn and pathetic lesson on the refining and spiritualising touch of death. Browne had watched the decline of his patient through the last lingering stages of consumption. As a physician, he noted the symptoms of that incurable disease. As a friend, he dwelt upon the ethereal serenity of the youth's soul. As a philosopher, he discussed divers opinions regarding the course and treatment of marasmus. But while digressing into general considerations, and enlarging upon the erudition of the subject, he ever returns with subtle instinct to the beauty of a natural but dreaded process, which purged the man, while yet alive, from earthly grossness, and made his final entrance into immortality but, as it were, the fading of a star of morning into light of day. Thus contemplated, the King of Terrors drops his dart, assuming the semblance of his brother Sleep. He becomes the purifier, the deliverer, the healer Thanatos Paian, the mystagogue of greater mysteries. The gradual attenuation of the body is a preparation for the soul's escape by gliding or absorption into unseen modes of life. At last the flesh becomes so thin and so diaphanous, that the spirit shines through it like flame in urns of alabaster. Then, with a sigh, the flame expires; but not as mortal flames, because the fuel which sustained them is exhausted. No: it has burned through its envelope of carnal tissue, and has exhaled, a disembodied ghost. This, or something like this, we feel when reading Sir Thomas Browne's epistle. But his style is so moderated, the suspension of his soul before the august spectacle of dying is so grave, his touch upon the mystery is at once so reverent and so familiar, his foresight of immortality is so far more felt than uttered, that any descant on the evenly-sustained and long-drawn theme impairs its weirdly unpremeditated influence.

This letter was first printed as a prelude to *Christian Morals*, another posthumous piece. Sir Thomas Browne himself indicated their juxta-position ; for he closed his epistle with a handful of hortatory apophthegms, which he afterwards worked up in the exordium to *Christian Morals*. That treatise is said to have been intended for a sequel to *Religio Medici*. Written in later life, his style has become more sententious, less discursive, less genially paradoxical. "The quick succession of images" which Dr. Johnson praised, have disap-peared. The didactic solemnity of Epictetus or Marcus Aurelius rules its inspiration rather than the self-complacent humour of Montaigne. The diction, too, shows signs of labour and of effort. Browne's hyperlatinism has become a vicious habit. He uses crude unaltered Latin words, like "compage," "confinium," "angustias." He talks of "vivacious abominations" and "longævous generations." He recommends a moderate caution in this portentous sentence: "Move circumspectly, not meticulously; and rather carefully solicitous than anxiously solicitudinous." Such phrases have the appearance of some caricature of the style in which *Religio Medici* was written. Were not the evidence for its genuineness convincing, we might fancy that *Christian Morals* were the work of an imitator rather than the mature production of so truly eloquent a writer. Yet we find many things in the book, which are in all points worthy of their author; and the whole is massy with condensed wisdom. Nothing could be nobler in sentiment or more pithy in expression than the following sentences, which I have culled at random:

Be substantially great in thyself, and more than thou appearest unto others; and let the world be deceived in thee, as they are in the lights of heaven.

Rest not in an ovation but a triumph over thy passions.

Let not the sun in Capricorn go down upon thy wrath, but write thy wrongs in ashes.

The world which took but six days to make, is like to take six thousand to make out.

The vices we scoff at in others laugh at us within ourselves.

The voice of prophecies is like that of whispering-places; they who are near, hear nothing; those at the farthest extremity will know all.

Futurity still shortens, and time present sucks in time to come.

The writings of Sir Thomas Browne will perhaps never become widely popular. As Spenser has been called the poet's poet, so we may call him the man-of-letters' prosaist. It requires a certain exercise of taste to apprehend his beauties, and a patience of the intellect to sympathise with his peculiar moods. He deals with obsolete and unfamiliar problems; he propounds riddles which no living Œdipus would care to solve; he ponders oftentimes on nugatory or fastidious questions, investing trifles with a dignity and splendour not their own. His noblest passages lie wedged like lumps of gold in masses of hard barren quartz; and the contemplations which awake his most ethereal fancy are such as few would pause to dwell upon. Wrecks of forgotten fables, antediluvian computations, names sculptured on the pyramids, or nameless urns consigned by hands unknown to alien soil, the influences of the stars, the occult potencies of herbs, interpretations of irrelevant dreams, fine disputations on theologies of schoolmen, conjectures of the soul's state before birth and after death—all things, in short, that are vague, impalpable, and charged with spiritual symbolism, this man loves to brood on. Round these topics his thought eddies like a dark and swirling stream. He spins sentence after sentence, and interweaves magnificent period with period, returning ever to the point wherefrom he started, dyeing the threads of his harmonious discourse in dim and shadowy colours which the dusky thought supplies. There is something inconclusive in the habit of his fancy, a delight in intellectual twilight, a moth-like flitting to and fro in regions where no certainty can be attained. On closing one of his laborious treatises, we feel that Morpheus has been leading us through labyrinths of dreams. Left at the end without a clue, suspense of judgment, puzzled by variety of detail, we are released from the magician's spell by a sudden dissolution of the vision and a gradual return into the world of facts. It is like awakening from the intoxication of hashish or of opium.

Whatever he was as a man and agent in the world, as a rhetorician he preferred the crepuscular limbo between attainable knowledge and irresolute conjecture. There he spread the downy, dimly-gorgeous wings of his imagination. While England was being torn with civil war, he pondered in his study upon Pharaoh, and the song the Sirens sang, and the name Achilles bore among the daughters of the King of Scyros. Still these remote and visionary cogitations did not distract him from the business and ambitions of the present. He had travelled in many parts of Europe, conversed with several sorts of men, and formed a practical philosophy from wide experience of human life. Therefore his most hazy speculations are shot with flashes of penetrative wisdom; and when we least demand them in his work, we light on epigrams of worldly prudence. Unexpectedness is a main source of his charm as a writer. There is a sustained paradox in his thought, which does not seem to have belonged to the man, so much as to the verbal artist. He professes a mixture of the boldest scepticism and the most puerile credulity. But his scepticism is the prelude to confessions of impassioned faith, and his credulity is the result of tortuous reflections on the enigmas of life and revelation. Perhaps the following paragraph enables us to understand the permanent temper of his mind most truly:

As for those wingy mysteries in divinity, and airy subtleties in religion, which have unhinged the brains of better heads, they never stretched the *pia mater* of mine. Methinks there be not impossibilities enough in religion for an active faith: the deepest mysteries ours contains have not only been illustrated but maintained by syllogism and the rule of reason. I love to lose myself in a mystery; to pursue my reason to an *O altitudo!* 'Tis my solitary recreation to pose my apprehension with those involved enigmas and riddles of the Trinity, Incarnation, and Resurrection. I can answer all the objections of Satan and my rebellious reason with that odd resolution I learned of Tertullian, *Certum est quia impossibile est.* I desire to exercise my faith in the difficultest point, for to credit ordinary and visible objects, is not faith, but persuasion.

Nothing short of an entire and impenetrable mystery will please him. He proceeds to thank God that he was not born in the age of miracles, for then his faith would have been an easy and common thing. His great regret is that he did not breathe this air before the days of Moses and of Christ; and he envies the patriarchs, for " they only had the advantage of a bold and noble faith who lived before His coming, who upon obscure prophecies and mystical types could raise a belief and expect apparent impossibilities." The creeds of the Apostles and Nicea and St. Athanasius are far too clear and simple for this aristocrat of belief, " nauseating *crambe* verities and questions over-queried," abhorring " flat and flexible truths,"

retiring with disgust from "vulgar speculations."
It is the same desire to escape from the palpable
and real into the vague and immaterial regions
of the intellect, which makes him give no other
reason for his contempt of reliques than that their
antiquity is not remote enough. The bones of St.
Peter or St. Mark are too close, forsooth, in time
to satisfy him. They win but vulgar credence,
having naught to exercise a select divinatory instinct. Mere age cannot perplex his fancy, which
loves to explore the recesses of the grave, and follow
spirits on their flight toward eternity. Yet, because
around the past there clings a shadowy mist of
unreality, he is wont to carry up his cogitations to
the beginning of the world. Methuselah is a name
often upon his lips, and the extreme age of an
opinion seems to him to be some warrant for its
truth. In the Garden of Eden he walks as though
he had been bred there, and reasons upon Adam's
thoughts with the familiarity of one who shared
his perplexities.

Sir Thomas Browne's brain was like a crucible
for reducing heterogeneous and various experience
to the potable gold of abstruse imagination. The
world he mostly thought of was the world of his
own mind; the material globe he used at times for
his recreation. When he affronts Death, he does
not dwell upon its terror or its calm, but records
his "abject conceit of this common way of existence,
this retaining to the sun and elements." The gor-
geous tombs and sculptured urns of princes make

him exclaim in scorn, that "to subsist in bones, and be but pyramidally extant, is a fallacy in duration" When he casts his eyes backward over years gone by, he sighs because "it is too late to be ambitious. The great mutations of the world are acted, or time may be too short for our designs." Between the world of facts and the world of dreams he sees no difference, except that perhaps the sleeping is more real than the waking. "There is an equal delusion in both, and the one doth but seem to be an emblem or picture of the other; we are somewhat more than ourselves in our sleep, and the slumber of the body seems to be but the waking of the soul." In measuring himself, he takes the universe for his standard: "The earth is a point, not only in respect of the heavens above us, but of that heavenly or celestial part within us. . . . That surface that tells the heavens it hath an end, cannot persuade me I have any." Although with obvious sincerity and feeling candour he assures us that he has no taint of pride, yet he stands thus haughtily upon the pedestal of human dignity: "There is surely a piece of divinity in us; something that was before the elements, and owes no homage unto the sun."

We need not wonder why a thinker of this stamp, to whom mystery was as the breath of his intellectual nostrils, and the apprehension of the divine in man and nature as his daily food, should have written: "Now for my life, it is a miracle of thirty years, which, to relate, were not a history, but a piece of poetry, and would sound to common ears like a fable." We need not speculate with Dr. Johnson what there could have been in the young physician's uneventful career to justify this " solemn assertion." Extremes meet, and Walt Whitman's " ever recurring miracle of the grass" tallies Sir Thomas Browne's enthusiastic contemplation of his manhood:

> To me, every hour of the light and dark is a miracle,
> Every inch of space is a miracle,
> Every spear of grass—the frames, limbs, organs, of
> men and women, and all that concerns them,
> All these to me are unspeakably perfect miracles.

This is the utterance of a mind cast in the same mystical, yet sanely realistic, mould as Sir Thomas Browne's. Only Browne retained something of exclusiveness, something derived from the past age of feudalism, a tincture of that humanistic conception of man's worth, which implied contempt for the illiterate vulgar. Browne was emphatically a mental aristocrat; and this perhaps may be transmitted to the reader as the surest key-word to his writings.

BORROW'S "WILD WALES"

By Theodore Watts-Dunton

Let me begin by saying that although the book is
an entirely worthy compeer of *Lavengro* and *The
Romany Rye*, and although like them it is written
in the autobiographic form, it belongs, as I propose
to show further on, to an entirely different form of
narrative from those two famous books. And it
differs in this respect even from *The Bible in Spain*.
Unlike that splendid book, it is just a simple, un-
coloured record of a walking tour through the
Principality. As in any other itinerary, events in
Wild Wales are depicted as they actually occurred,
enriched by none of that glamour in which Borrow
loved to disport himself. I remember once asking
him why in this book he wrote an autobiographic
narrative so fundamentally different from *Lavengro*
and *The Romany Rye*—why he had made in this
book none of those excursions into the realms of
fancy which form so charming a part of his famous
quasi-autobiographic narratives. It was entirely
characteristic of him that he remained silent as he
walked rather sulkily by my side. To find an answer
to the queries, however, is not very difficult. Making
a tour as he did on this occasion in the company
of eye-witnesses — eye-witnesses of an extremely

different temper from his own, eye-witnesses, more-over, whom he specially wished to satisfy and please —his wife and stepdaughter—he found it impossible to indulge in his bohemian proclivities and equally impossible to give his readers any of those romantic coincidences, those quaint arrangements of incidents to illustrate theories of life, which illuminate his other works. The tour was made in the summer and autumn of 1854; during the two or three years following, he seems to have been working upon this record of it. The book was announced for publication in 1857, but it was not until 1862 that his publisher, who had been so greatly disappointed by the reception given to *Lavengro* and *The Romany Rye*, took courage to offer it to the public.

In 1860 Borrow's interest in Wales and Welsh literature had specially been shown by the publication of his English version of *Gweledigaethau y Bardd Cwsg*, a curious kind of allegory in the form of a vision, written in the early years of the eighteenth century by a Welsh clergyman named Ellis Wynn. The English reader of Borrow's works will remember the allusion made to this book. As might have been expected, Borrow's translation of this Welsh prose classic is not very trustworthy, and it has been superseded by the translation of Mr. R. Gwyneddon Davies, published in 1897. A characteristic matter connected with Borrow's translation is that in the *Quarterly Review* for January 1861 he himself reviewed it anony-

mously, and not without appreciation of its merits
—a method which may be recommended to those
authors who are not in sympathy with their reviewers. The article showed a great deal of what
may be called Borrovian knowledge of the Welsh
language and Welsh literature, and perhaps it is
not ungenerous to say a good deal of Borrovian
ignorance too. For never was Nature's love of
whim in the fashioning of individuals more delightfully exemplified than in the case of Borrow's
irresistible desire for scholarship. Nothing whatever had he of the temperament of the true scholar
—nothing whatever of the philologist's endow-
ment, and yet to be recognised as a scholar was
the great ambitious dream of his life. I wish I had
time to compare his disquisitions upon the Welsh
language and literature in this article with a very
rare little book on the same subject, the *Sketch of
the History of the Welsh Language and Literature*,
by a remarkable man as entirely forgotten now as
Borrow is well remembered—Thomas Watts of
the British Museum. In the one case we get
nebulous speculation and fanciful induction based
upon Borrovian knowledge; in the other, a solid
mass of real learning accompanied by the smallest
possible amount of speculation or fanciful induction.

Borrow had a certain something of Mezzofanti's
prodigious memory for words, accompanied by the
great Italian's lack of philological science. It may
be remembered in this connection that Mr. Thomas
St. E. Hake in his reminiscences in *Notes and*

Queries of a relation of mine, the late Mr. James Orlando Watts, says that the learned recluse used to express a good deal of humorous contempt of Borrow's "method of learning languages from dictionaries only," without any grammatical knowledge. And these strictures, if we consider them, will explain much in regard to the philological disquisitions in *Lavengro*, *The Romany Rye*, and *Wild Wales*, where the knowledge is all " dictionary knowledge." But it was not the shaky philology that caused *Wild Wales* to fall almost dead from the press. What, then, was the cause ? It arose from the fact, as I hinted above, that *Wild Wales* belongs to a different kind of autobiographic narrative from *Lavengro* and *The Romany Rye*, and also, if the truth must be said, from *The Bible in Spain*.

At the period when Borrow wrote this book the great and vigorous renascence of the Cymric idea, the new and deep interest that Welshmen are now taking in the preservation of the Welsh tongue, had not begun. That Borrow did not live to this day, when Welsh is much more spoken among the cultivated class than in his time, is to be lamented. With regard to this revival, whatever may become of it (whether the Welsh language can really be made to survive in the great linguistic struggle for life, which will be one of the principal features of the twentieth century), no one will deny that it is a language which from the poetic side as well as from the historic ought to survive. If I tread here upon dangerous ground, I may yet venture to say that one great obstacle against the spread of the Welsh language beyond Wales is the strange orthography. It is difficult for a person unacquainted with Welsh to believe that the sounds represented by such awkward arrangements of consonants as Welsh displays are otherwise than unmusical. And yet as a matter of fact those sounds are very musical. It may be remarked here that there is another language spoken in Europe which suffers from the same misfortune in regard to phonetics—the Magyar language. I have elsewhere in a novel, whose scene is partly laid in Hungary, made a character speak of the disappointment expressed by the traveller in Central Europe, when crossing the Austrian frontier into Hungary by rail, at the sight of the Hungarian names with which the stations become suddenly placarded. German is an ugly-looking language enough, but in this respect it is nothing to the Hungarian. And yet it would be hard to find in the whole of Europe a more musical tongue than that which is represented by the uncouth consonantal syllables. It is not a little striking too that between the Cymric race and the Magyar race there are many points of likeness; one of these is the intense love of music displayed by the two, another is the blending of poetic imagination with practical sagacity. The Magyars have been called a race of lawyers, but their love of law-points and litigation is not greater than that of the Welsh, and yet how poetical is each race to the core!

With regard to languages—to survive will in the

present century mean to spread. Languages that do not spread will be crushed out. People who talk glibly about the vast expansion of the English language all over the world do not seem to realise that it is not the excellence of a tongue which makes it survive and causes it to spread over the earth, but the energy, military or commercial, of the people who speak it. It is not the excellence of the tongue of Shakespeare and Milton that has carried it all round the globe, but the busy energy of the common-place people who migrated for the most common-place ends imaginable, and took the language with them, and then increased and multiplied, building up new English-speaking communities. It is for this reason that the English language seems destined to become, if not the "universal language," at least the *lingua franca* of the world. And nothing is more pathetic than to observe the dread among Continental nations that this will be the case in the future; and nothing is more humorous than the passionate attempts to invent artificial languages, Volapük, Esperanto and what not, to do the work that the English language is already doing all over the sea, and will, apparently, soon be doing all over the land.

I dwell here upon this interesting subject in order to say that if Welsh does not survive it will not be because it is not a fine language, but simply because Destiny has decreed that it shall share the fate of many another language spoken at present much more widely than Welsh.

In speaking of any one of Borrow's books it is always necessary to say a good deal about Borrow as a man. Besides being the very child of Nature's fantasy, he was the prince of literary egotists. Everything in human life and everything in nature upon which he looked was enveloped in a coloured atmosphere shed by the eccentric ego. That his love of Wales was genuine there can be no doubt whatever. For this there was perhaps a very special reason—a reason quite unrecognised by himself. I have somewhere—but I forget where—remarked upon a curious and common mistake in regard to Borrow—I mean the mistake of speaking of him as an East Anglian. Very gratifying was this mistake to Borrow himself. When walking with me in Richmond Park, or elsewhere, he would frequently stop, look round and murmur, " Beautiful England! " and then begin to declare eloquently that there was not in the world a country to be compared with it, and that the race which lived in this beloved land was equally incomparable in most things, especially in what he valued so much— athleticism in all its forms. This was merely because England was his place of birth. Born in East Anglia he was, to be sure ; but Dr. Johnson long ago held to the opinion that a man born in a stable need not necessarily be described as a horse. When a man's father is pure Cornish (Celtic) and when his mother is mainly French, the fact of his having been born in Norfolk is not enough to make him an East Anglian. By an accident the regiment

to which his father belonged was located in Norfolk
at the time of his birth, just as by an accident it
might have been located in Ireland or Scotland.
In either of these cases he would have been George
Borrow the Celt, or rather George Borrow the
Unique, but not a Scotsman—not an Irishman. It
is the blood in a man's veins, it is not the spot in
which he is born, that decides the question of his
race. Does one call the daughters of the Irishman,
Patrick Brontë, who were Celtic to the marrow,
Yorkshire girls because they were born at Thorn-
ton? Does one call Mr. Swinburne a Londoner
because he, a Northumbrian by a long line of
ancestors, chanced to be born within a stone's-
throw of Belgrave Square? Does one call the
Rossettis Londoners because it was in London,
and not in Italy, that they were born? To imagine
any man more Celtic than Borrow is impossible.
Not a single East Anglian characteristic exhibited
by him do I remember—except perhaps his Norfolk
accent, and his very worthy and exemplary passion
for "boiled leg of mutton with turnips and caper
sauce," which he pronounced to be "food for the
gods." It was his own way of writing and talking
about himself, however, that fostered if it did not
originate the conception that Borrow was an East
Anglian. There is no more unreasonable, as there
is no more winsome, trait in human nature than
the form of egotism which I will call provincial
patriotism—a quality of which Borrow was so full.
No matter what unlovely spot in any country had

given Borrow birth, it would have become in his
eyes sanctified because of the all-important fact
that it gave birth to George Borrow, the "word-
master." Rest assured that had he been a fenman
he would have been as proud of his treeless, black-
earthed fen as he would have been proud of the
Swiss mountains had his birthplace chanced to be
Switzerland. Rest assured that had he been born
upon the barren soil of Damaraland he would have
been proud of his desert, as proud as he would have
been of any hilly district that had chanced to have
the honour of giving him birth. But being born
in East Anglia, to feel that he was the typical
Anglo-Saxon of all Anglo-Saxons around him gave
him a mighty joy. At " The Bald-faced Stag " his
eloquent addresses, to me and the little band of
friends who loved him, about Norfolk ale were
inspired by the same cause. Compared to that
East Anglian nectar all other nectars were " swipes."
I know East Anglia well; few men know it better
—few men love it better. I say emphatically that
a man more out of sympathy with the East Anglian
temperament never lived than he who wished to
be taken, and was taken, as the representative East
Anglian. Moreover, one very potent reason why
he was such a failure in Norfolk—one very potent
reason why he was such a failure in his contact
with the Anglo-Saxon race generally—was this: he
was a Celtic duckling hatched at Dereham, who
took himself for a veritable Norfolk chicken. It
is no wonder, therefore, that, without knowing it,

his sympathy with the Celt, especially the Cymric Celt, which he himself fully believed to be philological, was racial.

The scenery of Wales had a very especial appeal for him, and no wonder; for there is nothing like it in the world. Although I am familiar with the Alps and the other mountain ranges of Europe in their wildest and most beautiful recesses, it is with me as it was with Borrow: no hill scenery has the peculiar witchery of that around Eryri. It is unique in the scenery of Europe. Grander scenery there is on the Continent, no doubt—much grander—and scenery more soft and lovely; but none in which grandeur and loveliness meet and mingle in so fascinating a way as in Wales. Moreover, to Borrow, as to all lovers of Wild Wales, beautiful as its scenery is, it is the romantic associations of that scenery which form so large a portion of its charm. For what race in Europe has a story so poetic, so romantic, so pathetic as the Welsh? Over every inch of the Principality hovers that great Spirit who walks the earth hand in hand with his brother, the Spirit of Poetry, and throws a rainbow radiance over it—the Spirit of Antiquity. Upon this Borrow and the writer of these lines have often talked. No man ever felt more deeply than he that part and parcel of the very life of man is the atmosphere in which the Spirit of Antiquity lives. Irrational the sentiment about this Spirit may be, if you will, but stifled it will never be. Physical science strengthens rather than weakens the magical

glamour of the Spirit of Antiquity. Even the most
advanced social science, try to hate him as it may,
cannot dim his glory. To the beloved poet of the
socialists—William Morris—he was as dear, as
great and as strong as to the most conservative
poet that has ever lived. Those who express wonderment that in these days there should be the old
human playthings as bright and captivating as ever
—those who express wonderment at the survival
of all the delightful features of the old European
raree-show—have not realised the power of this
Spirit and the power of the sentiment about him.
What is the use of telling us that even in Grecian
annals there is no kind of heroism recorded which
you cannot match in the histories of modern
countries—even of new countries, such as the
United States and the Australias and Canada?
What is the use of telling us that the travels of
Ulysses and of Jason are as nothing in point of real
romance compared with Captain Phillip's voyage
to the other side of the world, when he led his
little convict-laden fleet to Botany Bay—a bay
then as unknown almost as any bay in Laputa—
that voyage which resulted in the founding of a
cluster of great nations any one of whose mammoth
millionaires could now buy up Ilium and the golden
fleece combined? The Spirit of Antiquity knows
not that captain, and hence the Spirit of Poetry
has nothing to say about him. In a thousand years'
time, no doubt, these things may be as ripe for
poetic treatment as the voyage of the Argonauts,

or the voyage of the Cymric Prince Madoc, who
the romantic lover of Wales, in spite of the arguments of Thomas Stephens, will still believe sailed
westward with his fleet and discovered America
before Columbus,—returned, and then sailed westward again into eternity. Now every peak and
cliff of Snowdonia, and every matchless valley and
dale of the land of the Druids, is very specially
beloved by the Spirit of Antiquity. The land of
Druidism—the land of that mysterious poetic
religion which more than any other religion expresses the very voice of Nature, is the land painted
in this delightful volume—Wild Wales. Compared
with Druidism, all other religious systems have a
sort of commonplace and modern ring, even those
which preceded it by centuries. The scenic witchery
of Wild Wales is great, no doubt, but it is enormously intensified by the memory of the heroic
struggle of the unconquerable remnant of the
ancient Britons with the brutal, physical power of
Roman and Saxon. The history of Wales is an epic
not to be surpassed for poetry and for romance.
And even these things did not comprise all the
points in connection with Wild Wales that delighted
Borrow. For when the student of Welsh history
and the lover of Welsh scenery is brought into
contact with the contemporary Welsh people, the
charm of the land does not fade, it is not fingered
away by personal contact: it is, indeed, augmented
tenfold. I have in *Aylwin* dwelt upon the poetry
of Welsh common life, the passionate love of the

Welsh people for a tiny strip of Welsh soil, the
religion of hearth and home, the devotion to wife
and children. In the Arvon edition of that book,
dedicated to a Welsh poet, I have said what I had
previously often said to Borrow, that, "although
I have seen a good deal of the races of Europe,
I put the Cymric race in many ways at the top
of them all. They combine, as I think, the poetry,
the music, the instinctive love of the fine arts, and
the humour of the other Celtic peoples with the
practicalness and bright-eyed sagacity of the very
different race to which they were so closely linked
by circumstance—the race whom it is the fashion
to call the Anglo-Saxon. And as to the charm of
the Welsh girls, no one who knows them as you
and I do can fail to be struck by it continually.
Winifred Wynne I meant to be the typical Welsh
girl as I have found her—affectionate, warm-
hearted, self-sacrificing and brave."

It seems almost necessary that in this desultory
talk upon *Wild Wales* I should, before proceeding
any further, say a few words upon the book in its
relations to two of Borrow's other autobiographic
narratives, *Lavengro* and *The Romany Rye*, and I
do not know any literary subject more suggestive
of interesting criticism.

Although Borrow always acknowledged **Defoe**
as his master, he had, of course, qualities of his
own that were as unlike Defoe's qualities as they
were unlike those of any other writer. And as

this speciality of his has, so far as I know, never been discussed, I should have liked, had space permitted, to give interest to my remarks upon *Wild Wales* by a thorough comparison between Borrow's imaginative works and Defoe's *Robinson Crusoe*. This is impossible in the space at my command. And yet a few words upon the subject I cannot resist indulging in, for it relates to the very core and central light of Borrow's genius; and I may now never have another opportunity of touching upon it.

I remember a long talk I once had with him upon the method of Defoe as contrasted and compared with his own method in *Lavengro*, *The Romany Rye*, and *Wild Wales*, and the method of other writers who adopt the autobiographic form of fiction. He agreed with me that the most successful of all stories in the autobiographic form is *Robinson Crusoe*, although *Jane Eyre*, *David Copperfield* and *Great Expectations* among English novels, and *Gil Blas* and *Manon Lescaut* among French novels, are also autobiographic in form. It is of all forms the most difficult. But its advantages, if they can be secured without making too many artistic sacrifices, are enormous. Flexibility is, of course, the one quality it lacks, but, lacking that, it cannot secure the variety of picture and the breadth of movement which is the special strength of the historic form.

The great pupils of Defoe—and by pupils I mean those writers who try to give as much common-

place ἀπάτη as possible to new and striking incidents
—Edgar Poe, Wilkie Collins, Gaboriau and others,
recognise the immense aid given to illusion by
adopting the autobiographic form.

The conversation upon this subject occurred in
one of my rambles with Borrow and Dr. Gordon
Hake in Richmond Park, when I had been pointing
out to the former certain passages in *Robinson
Crusoe* where Defoe adds richness and piquancy
to the incidents by making the reader believe that
these incidents will in the end have some deep
influence, spiritual or physical, upon the narrator
himself.

Borrow was not a theoriser, and yet he took a
quaint interest in other people's theorisings. He
asked me to explain myself more fully. My reply
in substance was something like this: Although in
Robinson Crusoe the autobiographer is really intro-
duced only to act as eye-witness for the purpose of
bringing out and authenticating the incidents of the
dramatic action, Defoe had the artistic craftiness to
make it appear that this was not so—to make it
appear that the incidents are selected by Crusoe in
such a way as to exhibit and develop the emotions
moving within his own breast. Defoe's *apparent*
object in writing the story was to show the effect of
a long solitude upon the human heart and mind ;
but it was not so—it was simply to bring into
fiction a series of incidents and adventures of
extraordinary interest and picturesqueness—incidents
such as did in part happen to Alexander Selkirk.

But Defoe was a much greater artist than he is generally credited with being, and he had sufficient of the artistic instinct to know that, interesting as these external incidents were in themselves, they could be made still more interesting by humanising them—by making it appear that they worked as a great life-lesson for the man who experienced them, and that this was why the man recorded them. Those moralisings of Crusoe upon the way in which the disasters of his life came upon him as " judgments," on account of his running away from his parents, seem to humanise the wheels of circumstance. They create in the reader's mind the interest in the man's personality which Defoe wished to create.

In reply to my criticism, Borrow said, " May not the same be said of Le Sage's *Gil Blas* ? "

And when I pointed out to him that there was a kind of kinship between the two writers in this particular he asked me to indicate in *Lavengro* and *The Romany Rye* such incidents in which Defoe's method had been followed by himself as had struck me. I pointed out several of them. Borrow, as a rule, was not at all given to frank discussion of his own artistic methods, indeed, he had a great deal of the instinct of the literary *histrio*—more than I have ever seen in any other writer—but he admitted that he had consciously in part and in part unconsciously adopted Defoe's method. The fact is, as I said to Borrow on that occasion, and as I have since had an opportunity of saying more fully in print, there are two kinds of autobiographic stories, and these two kinds are, if properly examined, really more unlike each other than the autobiographic form is unlike what is generally supposed to be its antithesis—the historic form. In one kind of autobiographic story, of which *Rob Roy* is a typical example, the narrator, though nominally the protagonist, is really not much more than the passive eye-witness of the dramatic action—not much more than the chorus to other characters who govern, or at least influence, the main issue. Inasmuch as he is an eye-witness of the dramatic action, he gives to it the authenticity of direct testimony. Through him the narrative gains a commonplace ἀπάτη such as is beyond the scope of the scattered forces of the historic form, howsoever powerfully handled. By the first-hand testimony of the eye-witness Frank Osbaldistone in Scott's fascinating novel, the more active characters, those who really control the main issue, Di Vernon, Rashleigh Osbaldistone, Rob, and Bailie Nicol Jarvie, are painted in much more vivid and much more authentic colours than the method of the historic form would allow.

It is in the nature of things that this kind of autobiographic fiction, howsoever strong may be the incidents, is not nearly so absorbing as is the other kind I am going to instance, the psychological, to which *Lavengro* and *The Romany Rye* belong; for in literature, as in life, the more interest we feel in the character, the more interest we feel in what befalls the character. Unlike the kind of autobiographic fiction typified by *Rob Roy*, in which, as I have said, the main issue is little influenced and not at all controlled by the narrator but by other characters, or, if not by other characters, by the wheels of circumstance;—in the psychological kind of autobiographic fiction, the personality of the narrator controls, or largely controls, the main issue of the dramatic action. In other words, the incidents in the latter kind of autobiographic fiction are selected and marshalled for the purpose of declaring the character of the narrator. The most superb exemplars of this kind of autobiographic narrative are stories which in all other respects are extremely unlike Borrow's—*Caleb Williams*, *Manon Lescaut*, *Jane Eyre*, and *Villette*.

A year or two ago I recurred to this subject in some comments I made upon some judgments of a well-known and admirable critic. I will take the liberty of referring here to one or two of the remarks I then made, for they seem to bear very directly upon Borrow's method as compared with Defoe's. The same artistic instinct which we see in Defoe and in Borrow's quasi-autobiographic work is exhibited by the Abbé Prévost in *Manon Lescaut*. The real object of the last-mentioned story (which, it will be remembered, is an episode in a much longer story) was to paint vivid pictures of the careless life of Paris at the period of the story, and especially to paint in vivid colours a kind of character which is essentially peculiar to Paris, the light-hearted, good-natured, unheeding *grisette*. But by making it appear that the incidents in Chevalier des Grieux's life are selected by him in order to show the effect of the life-lesson upon himself, Prévost gives to every incident the piquancy which properly belongs to this, the psychological form of autobiographic fiction. It must, however, be admitted that at its best the autobiographic form of fiction is rarely, very rarely, broad enough to be a satisfactory form of art, even when, as in *The Woman in White*, the story consists of a series of autobiographic narratives stitched together. It was this difficulty which confronted Dickens when he wrote *Bleak House*. When he was writing *David Copperfield* he had felt the sweetness and fascination of writing in the autobiographic form, and had seen the sweetness and fascination of reading it; but he also felt how constricted the form is in regard to breadth, and it occurred to him that he could combine the two forms—that he could give in the same book the sweetness and the fascination and the authenticity of the autobiographic form and the breadth and variety of the historic form. To bring into an autobiographic narrative the complex and wide-spreading net that forms the story of *Bleak House* was, of course, impossible, and so he mixed up the chapters of Esther Summerson's autobiographic narrative with chapters of the history of the great Chancery suit and all that flowed from it. In order to minimise as much as possible the confusion of so very confused a scheme as this, he wrote the historic part of the book in the present tense; and the result is the most oppressively-laboured novel that was ever produced by a great novelist.

I have dwelt at length upon this subject because if I were asked to name one of the greatest masters of the autobiographic form, in any language, I should, I think, have to name Borrow. In one variety of that form he gave us *Lavengro* and *The Romany Rye*, in the other *Wild Wales*.

Wild Wales seems to have disappointed Borrovians because it ignores the Welsh gypsies, the most superior branch of all the Romany race, except, perhaps, the gypsy musicians of Hungary. And certainly it is curious to speculate as to why he ignores them in that fashion. Readers of *The Romany Rye* wonder why, after his adventure with Mrs. Herne and her granddaughter, and his rescue by the Welshman, Peter Williams, on reaching the Welsh border, Borrow kept his mouth closed. Several reasons have occurred to me, one of which is that his knowledge of Welsh Romany was of the shakiest kind. Another reason might have been that in *The Romany Rye*, as much of his story as could be told in two volumes being told, he abruptly broke off as he had broken off at the end of the third volume of *Lavengro*. Or did the same reason that caused him to write, in *Wild Wales*, an autobiographic narrative without any of the fantasies and romantic ornamentation which did so much to win popularity for his previous books, govern him when he decided to ignore the gypsies—the

presence of his wife and stepdaughter ? There is a
very wide class, including indeed the whole of
British Philistia, that cherishes a positive racial
aversion to the Romany—an aversion as strong as
the Russian aversion to the Jew.

Anyhow, it was very eccentric to write a book
upon Wales and to ignore so picturesque a feature
of the subject as the Welsh gypsies. For, beyond
doubt, the finest specimens of the Romany race
are—or were in Borrow's time—to be found in
Wales. And here I cannot help saying parentheti-
cally, that as Borrow gave us no word about the
Welsh Romanies and their language, the work of
Mr. Sampson, the greatest master of the Welsh
Romany that ever lived, is especially precious. So
great is the work of that admirable scholar upon
the subject that he told me when I last saw him that
he was actually translating Omar Khayyám into
Welsh Romany! Although the Welsh gypsies have
a much greater knowledge of Welsh Romany than
English gypsies have of English Romany, and
are more intelligent, I am a little sceptical, as
I told him, as to the Welsh Romanies taking that
deep interest in the immortal quatrains which, it
seems, atheists and Christians agree in doing among
the gorgios.

Those who have seen much of the writing frater-
nity of London or Paris, know that the great mass
of authors, whether in prose or in verse, have just
as much and just as little individuality—have just

as much and just as little of any new and true personal accent, as the vast flock of human sheep whose bleatings will soon drown all other voices over land and sea. They have the peculiar instinct for putting their thoughts into written words— that is all. This it is that makes Borrow such a memorable figure. If ever a man had an accent of his own that man was he. What that accent was I have tried to indicate here, in the remarks upon his method of writing autobiographic fiction. Vanity can make all, even the most cunning, simple on one side of their characters, but it made of Borrow a veritable child.

If Tennyson may be accepted as the type of the man without guile, what type does Borrow represent? In him guile and simplicity were blent in what must have been the most whimsical amalgam of opposite qualities ever seen on this planet. Let me give one instance out of a thousand of this.

Great as was his love of Wales and the Welsh, the Anglo-Saxonism—the John Bullism which he fondly cherished in that Celtic bosom of his, was so strong that whenever it came to pitting the prowess and the glories of the Welshman against those of the Englishman, his championship of the Cymric race would straightway vanish, and the claim of the Anglo-Saxon to superiority would be proclaimed against all the opposition of the world. This was especially so in regard to athletics, as was but natural, seeing that he always felt himself to be an athlete first, a writing man afterwards.

A favourite quotation of his was from Byron:

One hates an author that's *all author*—fellows
In foolscap uniforms turned up with ink.

Frederick Sandys, a Norfolk man who knew him well, rarely spoke of Borrow save as a master in the noble art of self-defence.

It was as a swimmer I first saw him—one of the strongest and hardiest that ever rejoiced to buffet with wintry billows on the Norfolk coast. And to the very last did his interest in swimming, sparring, running, wrestling, jumping remain. If the Welshman would only have admitted that in athletics the Englishman stands first—stands easily first among the competitors of the world, he would have cheerfully admitted that the Welshman made a good second. General Picton used to affirm that the ideal—the topmost soldier in the world is a Welshman of five feet eight inches in height. Such a man as the six-feet-three giant of Dereham knew well how to scorn such an assertion even though made by the great Picton himself. But suppose Borrow had been told, as we have lately been told, that the so-called "English archers" at Crecy and Agincourt were mainly made up of Welshmen, what a flush would have overspread his hairless cheek, what an indignant fire would have blazed from his eyes! Not even his indignation on being told, as we would sometimes tell him at "The Bald-faced Stag," that Scottish Highlanders had proved themselves superior to their English brothers-in-arms would have equalled his scorn of such talk about Crecy and Agincourt—scenes of English prowess that he was never tired of extolling.

But you had only to admit that Welshmen were superior to all others save Englishmen in physical prowess, and Borrow's championship of the Cymric athlete could be as enthusiastic and even as aggressive as the best and most self-assertive Welshman ever born in Arvon. Consequently I can but regret that he did not live to see the great recrudescence of Cymric energy which we are seeing at the present moment in " Cymru, gwlad y gân,"—an energy which is declaring itself more vigorously every day, and not merely in pure intellectual matters, not merely in political matters, but equally in those same athletics which to Borrow were so important. Sparring has gone out of fashion as much in the Principality as in England and Scotland; but that which has succeeded it, football, has taken a place in athleticism such as would have bewildered Borrow, as it would have bewildered most of his contemporaries. What would he have said, I wonder, had he been told that in this favourite twentieth-century game the Welsh would surpass all others in these islands, and save the honour of Great Britain? No one would have enjoyed wit-nessing the great contest between the Welsh and the New Zealand athletes at the Cardiff Arms Park on the 16th of last December with more gusto than the admirer of English sparring and of the English pugilistic heroes, from Big Ben Bryan

to Tom Spring. No one would have been more ex-
hilarated than he by the song with which it opened:

Mae hen wlad fy nhadau yn anwyl i mi.[1]

But one wonders what he would have said after
the struggle was over—after Wales's latest triumph
over the Saxon record of physical prowess. One
can imagine, perhaps, his mixed feelings had he
been a witness of that great athletic struggle which
is going to be historic—the immortal contest in
which after England had succumbed entirely to the
Colonials, the honour of the old country was saved
by Wales at the eleventh hour. His cheek would
have glowed with admiration of the exploits of the
only footballers whose names will be historic, and
being historic must be mentioned in connection
with his own Welsh pages,—I mean the names of
Travers, of Bush, of Winfield, of Owen, of Jones,
of Llewellyn, of Gabe, of Nicholls, of Morgan, of
Williams, of Hodges, of Harding, of Joseph, and
the names of the two Pritchards. Whatsoever
might have been his after-emotions when provincial patriotism began to assert itself, Borrow
would in that great hour of Cymric triumph have
frankly admitted, I think, that for once England's
honour was saved by Wales.

[1] The old land of my father is dear unto me.

ON THE ESSAYS OF ELIA

By the Rt. Hon. Augustine Birrell

No apology is needed, and certainly no preface is required, for or to *The Essays of Elia*. They have, to use their author's own words, joined the class of "perpetually self-reproductive volumes, Great Nature's Stereotypes." All that an editor of them has to do is to see that work so delicate, so conscientious, so elaborate, is neither insulted with bad type or ill-tempered paper, nor injured by careless printing. Having done this, he has done his duty. There is no need to praise what all the world praises. Sometimes (it is just possible) an author may slip his hold on men's fancies and fall into a state of neglect, and, so far as human memories are concerned, of ruinous decay, which yet may be removed, and the author's fame judiciously restored by the kindly enthusiasm of some critic, at whose bidding we turn to the forgotten volumes, and try to make up for past neglect by present rapture. But this (it must be owned) is rare. There are, indeed, more discoverers than discoveries; more bold travellers than new continents; more critics dinning the air with their joyful shouts over forgotten poets and disused dramatists than there prove to be poets and dramatists whom it is good to remember, or possible to use. These recovered creatures lead but a blinking kind of existence for a very short time, and then, even though their works may have been reprinted on Whatman paper, sink back into oblivion, and rest for ever on the shelves of that great library, the pride of Limbo, which is made up of the books that no man can read, even though he were to be paid for doing so. This repose is not unkindly. An author who is entirely forgotten is, at all events, never mispraised. Nothing, we may feel well assured, could cause the Author of *The Essays of Elia* more genuine annoyance than to be clumsily praised, or raised with shouting to a higher pedestal than the one in the possession of which his own ripe judgment could confirm him. And yet, if we are not to praise *The Essays of Elia*, what is there for us to do? And who can insure us against doing so clumsily? Happily it is not necessary to praise them at all.

The lives of authors, if only written with a decent measure of truthfulness and insight, are, generally speaking, better reading than their works. It would be hard to explain why the lives of men so querulous, so affected, so centred in self, so averse to the probing of criticism, so blind to the smallness of their fame as most authors stand revealed in their biographies and letters to have been, should yet be so incessantly interesting. They succeed one another quickly enough—these biographies; doing each one of them its bit of iconoclastic work: yet the reader never tires of them, nor, unless he is very young, does he wreak an empty wrath upon the fragments of another broken idol. Far otherwise: he picks up the pieces reverently, and remembering how hard and self-engrossing is the labour of carrying out any high plan of literary excellence, how furious the fever occasioned by the thought of perfection, how hot the hell of failure,—puts them carefully away, and thanks God his mother bore him as destitute of genius as of clothing.

But none the less we pine after the ideal. We want our favourite authors to be our best-loved men. Smashing idols is an irreverent occupation endurable only in our wilder hours. A time comes in most men's lives when the bell rings for prayer, and unhappy are they who, when it does, have nowhere to carry their heart's supplications.

It is, therefore, a pleasant thing when we find ourselves saying of Charles Lamb, that it is impossible to know whether we most admire the author, or love the man. The imaginary Elia, sitting by the side of his Cousin Bridget, playing sick whist, whilst the pipkin which was to prepare a gentle lenitive for his foot is bubbling in the fire, " and as I do not much relish appliances, there it should ever bubble—Bridget and I should be for ever playing," makes a picture which will never need retouching; but when we read in the *Life and Letters* how reality outdoes imagination, and learn that the pen of Elia, so wisely human, so sweetly melancholy, told only but a few of the secrets of a brave heart and an unselfish life, we feel we have saved something out of the wreck.

Lamb, like his own child-angel, was " to know weakness, and reliance, and the shadow of human imbecility." He went with a lame gait. He used to get drunk somewhat too frequently. Let the fact be stated in all its deformity—he was too fond of gin-and-water. He once gave a lady the welcome assurance that he never got drunk twice in the same house. Failing all evidence to the contrary, we are bound to believe this to be true. It is a mitigating circumstance. Wordsworth's boundless self-conceit, Coleridge's maddening infirmity of purpose, Hazlitt's petulance, De Quincey's spitefulness, knew no such self-denying ordinance. Lamb was also a too inveterate punster, and sometimes, it may be, pushed a jest, or baited a bore, beyond the limits of becoming mirth. When we have said these things against Lamb we have said all. Pale Malice, speckled Jealousy, may now be invited to search the records of his life, to probe his motives, to read his private letters, to pry into his desk, to dissect his character. Baffled, beaten, and disappointed, they fall back. An occasional intoxication which hurt no one but himself, which blinded him to no duty, which led him into no extravagance, which in no way interfered with the soundness of his judgment, the charity of his heart, or the independence of his life, and a shower of bad puns—

behold the faults of Elia! His virtues—noble, manly, gentle—are strewn over every page of his life, and may be read in every letter he ever wrote.

Charles Lamb was born in Crown Office Row, in the Temple, on the 18th of February, 1775. His father, John Lamb, was a barrister's clerk. The lots of barristers' clerks vary as widely as the habits of their employers. Some make fortunes for themselves; others only tea for their masters. Their success in life is not wholly dependent upon their own exertions. Rewarded as they are by a kind of parasitical fee growing out of those paid to the barrister they serve, they wax or wane— grow fat or lean along with their chief. Theirs is thus a double dependence. From a herd of the newly-called, how is the fledgling clerk to single out a Scott, a Palmer, or a Cairns? John Lamb was clerk to Mr. Samuel Salt, who, albeit a Bencher of his Inn, does not seem ever to have enjoyed, if that be the right word, a practice in the Courts. You may search the Law Reports of his period in vain for his name. The duties of John Lamb were rather those of a private secretary, or confidential upper servant, than of a barrister's clerk, properly so called. He collected his master's dividends— a more gentlemanlike occupation than dunning attornies for fees, marked but not paid. Salt was a man of ample fortune and of kind heart. He is immortalised in the Essay on "Some of the Old Benchers of the Inner Temple." It was he who procured for Charles a nomination to Christ's

Hospital, whither the boy proceeded on the 9th of October, 1782, and where he remained until November, 1789, when he left school for good, being then only in his fifteenth year. At Christ's Lamb received a purely classical education of the old-fashioned type. "In everything that relates to *science*," so he writes with obvious truthfulness, "I am a whole encyclopædia behind the rest of the world. I should scarcely have cut a figure amongst the franklins or country gentlemen in King John's days. I know less geography than a schoolboy of six weeks' standing. To me a map of old Ortelius is as authentic as Arrowsmith. I do not know whereabout Africa merges into Asia; whether Ethiopia lies in one or other of those great divisions; nor can form the remotest conjecture of the position of New South Wales or Van Diemen's Land." A civil servant of to-day could hardly afford to make such pleasant confessions. No boy ever profited more, or lost less, by an old-fashioned education than Lamb. His head, so he tells us, had not many mansions, nor spacious, but he had imagination, taste, and spirit, and he imbibed the old humanities at every pore. He never could have written *The Essays of Elia*, or anything like them, had he been robbed of the birthright of every man of letters. He is not a cheap and easy author. Leaving school as he did before he was fifteen, he never proceeded beyond the vestibules of the ancient learning; and this, perhaps, was also well. His stutter saved him from the

Universities, and he was thus enabled through life
to preserve a romantic attachment for these semin-
aries of sound learning and true religion. Literature
has no reason to deplore that Lamb never, save
in his imagination, proceeded a Master of Arts.
Some portion—it would be impossible to say what
—of his charm proceeds from the fact of his having
been a lettered clerk in the mercantile rather than
the ecclesiastical sense of the term. He has thus
become the patron saint, the inspiring example,
of those whom fate, perhaps not so unkind as she
seems, has condemned to know "the irksome
confinement of an office," and who have left to
them but the shreds and patches of the day for the
pursuits in which their souls rejoice.

After leaving Christ's Lamb spent a little more
than two years in the South Sea House, where his
elder and only brother John had a clerkship; but
in April 1792, through the influence probably
of Mr. Salt, he obtained a place in the Accountant's
Office of the East India Company, at whose desks
he sat until 1825, when, to use his own celebrated
phrase, he went home—for ever. His salary went
on slowly increasing from something under £100
to £600 a year. Apart from the old and probably
fictitious story about his coming late and going
home proportionately early, there is no reason to
suppose that Lamb was otherwise than an efficient
public servant, as that class of person goes. He did
no more than was expected of him, and had no
scruples about conducting his private correspond-

ence on office paper. He wrote a very clear hand, and was in all business matters a precise and punctual person. His code of honour was the highest, and through life he maintained a curious and passionate hatred of bankrupts.

He had been three years in the service of the Company when the great tragedy—Elizabethan in its horror—of his life befell him. Old John Lamb and his wife, their daughter Mary, an aunt, and Charles, were living huddled together in an obscure lodging in Little Queen Street, Holborn. An exceedingly ugly church now stands upon the site of the houses. Mary Lamb, who was ten years her younger brother's senior, was a dressmaker on a small scale. She always had what her mother, who does not seem greatly to have cared for her, called "moithered" brains, and on this fateful day, the 23rd of September, 1796, just before dinner, she seized a case-knife which was lying on the table, and pursued a little girl, her apprentice, round the room, hurled about the dinner-forks and finally stabbed her mother to the heart. When Charles came into the room, and snatched the knife out of her hand, it was to find his aunt lying apparently dying, his father with a wound on his forehead, and his mother a murdered corpse. He was then twenty-one years of age, and had spent some weeks of this very year in the Hoxton Lunatic Asylum. His elder brother John, who had a comfortable place in the South Sea House, did nothing but look after his own leg, which one is thankful to believe gave him a good deal of pain. The whole weight of the family fell upon Charles. His love for his sister manifested itself in his determination that as soon as possible she should be released from confinement and live at home, he undertaking ever to be on the watch for the fits of frenzy he was assured only too truthfully would necessarily be recurrent. For his father and his aunt, so long as they lived, he maintained a home. Poor Mary in her asylum was often heard to say that she had one brother who wished her to remain all her days in a madhouse, but another who would no have it so. Charles succeeded in obtaining her discharge upon entering into a solemn undertaking to take care of her for ever thereafter. At first he provided lodgings for her at Hackney, and spent all his Sundays and holidays with her, but soon after he took her to live with him altogether. Mr. Procter (Barry Cornwall), from whose account the above facts are taken in their entirety, says: "Whenever the approach of one of her fits of insanity was announced by some irritability or change of manner, he would take her under his arm to Hoxton Asylum. It was very affecting to encounter the young brother and sister walking together (weeping) on this painful errand, Mary herself, although sad, very conscious of the necessity of a temporary separation from her only friend. They used to carry a strait waistcoat with them."

These terrible events for a time greatly quickened the religious side of Lamb's character. His letters to Coleridge are severe, ascetical. He forswore poetry and amusements, even such as were in the reach of a poor boy of twenty-one maintaining a household on an income of £180. This wore off, and Lamb became in men's hasty judgments one of the profane—a trifler, a jester. Carlyle, we know only too well, met him once, and dismissed him with a sulphureous snort. My belief is that Lamb, feeling his own mental infirmity, and aware of the fearful life-long strain to which he was to be subjected, took refuge in trifles seriously, and played the fool in order to remain sane.

For many long years Charles and Mary Lamb lived together on narrow means and humble surroundings. Friends indeed they had—Wordsworth, Coleridge, Hazlitt, Manning, Rickman, Barton, Burney, Carey—of whom anyone might be proud. Their poverty was of the noble order. In manly independence he towers above his contemporaries. He hated a close bargain almost as much as he did a bankrupt. Prudent and saving, he could be generous and (as it is called) princely when occasion arose. He was ever a helper, seldom one of the helped. Both he and his sister eked out their slender means by literary work, humble in design, but honest in accomplishment. Save for the newspapers, to which Charles contributed doleful jests, they wrote nothing save their best.

In 1818, when Lamb's poetry and prose was collected and dignified, much to his amusement, with the title *Works,* he became more widely known, and was recognised, by at all events a few, as a man with a gift. In 1820 *The London Magazine* was established, and in its columns first appeared *The Essays of Elia*. In 1823 the first series appeared in a separate volume, and ten years later the last Essays.

The joint lives of Charles and Mary Lamb are best read in the former's letters, though Canon Ainger's *Life* should be kept by their side.

It was the wish of both that Charles should be the survivor; he would thus have seen his task complete. But it was not to be. He died at Edmonton on the 27th of December, 1834; Mary lived on till the 20th of May, 1847,—weary years, spent for the most part under the care of a nurse, and with but a "twilight of consciousness." Lamb had saved £2000, which, after his sister's life-interest ceased, was vested in trustees for the benefit of Mrs. Moxon, whom Mary and he had in a kind of way adopted.

IZAAK WALTON

By Andrew Lang

THE few events in the long life of Izaak Walton have been carefully investigated by Sir Harris Nicolas. All that can be extricated from documents by the alchemy of research has been selected, and I am unaware of any important acquisitions since Sir Harris Nicolas's second edition of 1860. Izaak was of an old family of Staffordshire yeomen, probably descendants of George Walton of Yoxhall, who died in 1571. Izaak's father was Jarvis Walton, who died in February 1595-6; of Izaak's mother nothing is known. Izaak himself was born at Stafford, on 9th August, 1593, and was baptised on 21st September. He died on 15th December, 1683, having lived in the reigns of Elizabeth, James I., Charles I., under the Commonwealth, and under Charles II. The anxious and changeful age through which he passed is in contrast with his very pacific character and tranquil pursuits.

Of Walton's education nothing is known, except on the evidence of his writings. He may have read Latin, but most of the books he cites had English translations. Did he learn his religion from " his mother or his nurse "? It will be seen that the

free speculation of his age left him untouched:
perhaps his piety was awakened, from childhood,
under the instruction of a pious mother. Had he
been orphaned of both parents (as has been suggested) he might have been less amenable to authority, and a less notable example of the virtues which
Anglicanism so vainly opposed to Puritanism. His
literary beginnings are obscure. There exists a copy
of a work, *The Loves of Amos and Laura*, written
by S. P., published in 1613, and again in 1619.
The edition of 1619 is dedicated to " Iz. Wa.":

> Thou being cause *it is as now it is;*

the Dedication does not occur in the one imperfect
known copy of 1613. Conceivably the words " as
now it is " refer to the edition of 1619, which might
have been emended by Walton's advice. But there
are no emendations, hence it is more probable that
Walton revised the poem in 1613, when he was
a man of twenty, or that he merely advised the
author to publish:

> For, hadst thou held thy tongue, by silence might
> These have been buried in oblivion's night.

S. P. also remarks:

> No ill thing can be clothed in thy verse;

hence Izaak was already a rhymer, and a harmless
one, under the Royal Prentice, gentle King Jamie.

By this time Walton was probably settled in
London. A deed in the possession of his biographer, Dr. Johnson's friend, Sir John Hawkins,
shows that, in 1614, Walton held half of a shop

on the north side of Fleet Street, two doors west of Chancery Lane: the other occupant was a hosier. Mr. Nicoll has discovered that Walton was made free of the Ironmongers' Company on 12th November, 1618. He is styled an Ironmonger in his marriage licence. The facts are given in Mr. Marston's Life of Walton, prefixed to his edition of *The Compleat Angler* (1888). It is odd that a prentice ironmonger should have been a poet and a critic of poetry. Dr. Donne, before 1614, was Vicar of St. Dunstan's in the West, and in Walton had a parishioner, a disciple, and a friend. Izaak greatly loved the society of the clergy: he connected himself with Episcopal families, and had a natural taste for a bishop. Through Donne, perhaps, or it may be in converse across the counter, he made acquaintance with Hales of Eton, Dr. King, and Sir Henry Wotton, himself an angler, and one who, like Donne and Izaak, loved a ghost story, and had several in his family. Drayton, the river-poet, author of the *Polyolbion*, is also spoken of by Walton as " my old deceased friend."

On 27th December, 1626, Walton married, at Canterbury, Rachel Floud, a niece, on the maternal side, by several descents, of Cranmer, the famous Archbishop of Canterbury. The Cranmers were intimate with the family of the judicious Hooker, and Walton was again connected with kinsfolk of that celebrated divine. Donne died in 1631, leaving to Walton, and to other friends, a bloodstone engraved with Christ crucified on an anchor: the seal is impressed on Walton's will. When Donne's poems were published in 1633, Walton added commendatory verses:

As all lament
(Or should) this general cause of discontent.

The parenthetic " or should " is much in Walton's manner. "Witness my mild pen, not used to upbraid the world," is also a pleasant and accurate piece of self-criticism. " I am his convert," Walton exclaims. In a citation from a manuscript which cannot be found, and perhaps never existed, Walton is spoken of as "a very sweet poet in his youth, and more than all in matters of love." Donne had been in the same case: he, or Time, may have converted Walton from amorous ditties. Walton, in an edition of Donne's poems of 1635, writes of

This book (dry emblem) which begins
With love; but ends with tears and sighs for sins.

The preacher and his convert had probably a similar history of the heart: as we shall see, Walton, like the Cyclops, had known love. Early in 1639, Wotton wrote to Walton about a proposed Life of Donne, to be written by himself, and hoped " to enjoy your own ever welcome company in the approaching time of the *Fly* and the *Cork*." Wotton was a fly-fisher; the cork, or float, or " trembling quill," marks Izaak for the bottom-fisher he was. Wotton died in December 1639; Walton prefixed his own Life of Donne to that divine's sermons in 1640. He says, in the Dedication of the reprint of 1658, that " it had the approbation of our

late learned and eloquent King," the martyred
Charles I. Living in, or at the corner of, Chancery Lane, Walton is known to have held parochial
office: he was even elected "scavenger." He had
the misfortune to lose seven children—of whom the
last died in 1641—his wife, and his mother-in-law.
In 1644 he left Chancery Lane, and probably
retired from trade. He was, of course, a Royalist.
Speaking of the entry of the Scots, who came, as
one of them said, " for the goods,—and chattels of
the English," he remarks, " I saw and suffered by
it." [1] He also mentions that he "saw" shops shut
by their owners till Laud should be put to death,
in January 1645. In his Life of Sanderson, Walton
vouches for an anecdote of " the knowing and conscientious King," Charles, who, he says, meant to
do public penance for Strafford's death, and for the
abolishing of Episcopacy in Scotland. But the condition, " peaceable possession of the Crown," was
not granted to Charles, nor could have been granted
to a prince who wished to reintroduce bishops in
Scotland. Walton had his information from Dr.
Morley. On 25th November, 1645, Walton
probably wrote, though John Marriott signed, an
Address to the Reader, printed, in 1646, with
Quarles's *Shepherd's Eclogues*. The piece is a little
idyll in prose, and "angle, lines, and flies" are not
omitted in the description of "the fruitful month
of May," while Pan is implored to restore Arcadian

---

[1] The quip about "goods and chattels" was revived
later, in the case of a royal mistress.

ANDREW LANG

peace to Britannia, "and grant that each honest
shepherd may again sit under his own vine and
fig-tree, and feed his own flock," when the king
comes, no doubt. "About" 1646 Walton married
Anne, half-sister of Bishop Ken, a lady "of much
Christian meeknesse." Sir Harris Nicolas thinks
that he only visited Stafford occasionally, in these
troubled years. He mentions fishing in "Shawford
brook"; he was likely to fish wherever there was
water, and the brook flowed through land which,
as Mr. Marston shows, he acquired about 1656.
In 1650 a child was born to Walton in Clerken-
well; it died, but another, Izaak, was born in September 1651. In 1651 he published the *Reliquiæ
Wottonianæ*, with a memoir of Sir Henry Wotton.
The knight had valued Walton's company as a
cure for "those splenetic vapours that are called
hypochondriacal."

Worcester fight was on 3rd September, 1651;
the king was defeated, and fled, escaping, thanks
to a stand made by Wogan, and to the loyalty of
Mistress Jane Lane, and of many other faithful
adherents. A jewel of Charles's, the lesser George,
was preserved by Colonel Blague, who intrusted it to
Mr. Barlow of Blore Pipe House, in Staffordshire.
Mr. Barlow gave it to Mr. Milward, a Royalist
prisoner in Stafford, and he, in turn, intrusted it
to Walton, who managed to convey it to Colonel
Blague in the Tower. The colonel escaped and
the George was given back to the king. Ashmole,
who tells the story, mentions Walton as "well

beloved of all good men." This incident is, perhaps, the only known adventure in the long life of old Izaak. The peaceful angler, with a royal jewel in his pocket, must have encountered many dangers on the highway. He was a man of sixty when he published his *Compleat Angler* in 1653, and so secured immortality. The quiet beauties of his manner in his various biographies would only have made him known to a few students, who could never have recognised Byron's " quaint, old, cruel coxcomb " in their author. " The whole discourse is a kind of picture of my own disposition, at least of my disposition in such days and times as I allow myself when honest Nat. and R. R. and I go a-fishing together." Izaak speaks of the possibility that his book may reach a second edition. There are now editions more than a hundred! Waltonians should read Mr. Thomas Westwood's Preface to his *Chronicle of the Compleat Angler*: it is reprinted in Mr. Marston's edition. Mr. Westwood learned to admire Walton at the feet of Charles Lamb:

> No fisher,
> But a well-wisher
> To the game,

as Scott describes himself.[1]

[1] Sir Walter was fond of trout-fishing, and in his *Quarterly* review of Davy's *Salmonia*, describes his pleasure in wading Tweed, in "Tom Fool's light" at the end of a hot summer day. In salmon-fishing he was no expert, and said to Lockhart that he must have Tom Purdie to aid him in his review of *Salmonia*. The picturesqueness of salmon-spearing by torchlight seduced Scott from the legitimate sport.

Lamb recommended Walton to Coleridge: " it breathes the very spirit of innocence, purity, and simplicity of heart; . . . it would sweeten a man's temper at any time to read it; it would Christianise every angry, discordant passion; pray make yourself acquainted with it." (28th October, 1796.) According to Mr. Westwood, Lamb had " an early copy," found in a repository of marine stores, but not, even then, to be bought at a bargain. Mr. Westwood fears that Lamb's copy was only Hawkins's edition of 1760. The original is extremely scarce. Mr. Locker had a fine copy; there is another in the library of Dorchester House: both are in their primitive livery of brown sheep, or calf. The book is one which only the wealthy collector can hope, with luck, to call his own. A small octavo, sold at eighteenpence, *The Compleat Angler* was certain to be thumbed into nothingness, after enduring much from May showers, July suns, and fishy companionship. It is almost a wonder that any examples of Walton's and Bunyan's first editions have survived into our day. The little volume was meant to find a place in the bulging pockets of anglers, and was well adapted to that end. The work should be reprinted in a similar *format*: quarto editions are out of place.

The fortunes of the book, the *fata libelli*, have been traced by Mr. Westwood. There are several misprints (later corrected) in the earliest copies, as (p. 88) " Fordig " for " Fordidg," (p. 152) " Pudoch " for " Pudock." The appearance of the work was advertised in *The Perfect Diurnal* (9-16th May), and in No. 154 of *The Mercurius Politicus* (19-26th May), also in an almanac for 1654. Izaak, or his publisher Marriott, cunningly brought out the book at a season when men expect the Mayfly. Just a month before, Oliver Cromwell had walked into the House of Commons, in a plain suit of black clothes, with grey stockings. His language, when he spoke, was reckoned unparliamentary (as it undeniably was), and he dissolved the Long Parliament. While Marriott was advertising Walton's work, Cromwell was making a Parliament of Saints, "faithful, fearing God, and hating covetousness." This is a good description of Izaak, but he was not selected. In the midst of revolutions came *The Compleat Angler* to the light, a possession for ever. Its original purchasers are not likely to have taken a hand in Royalist plots or saintly conventicles. They were peaceful men. A certain Cromwellian trooper, Richard Franck, was a better angler than Walton, and he has left to us the only contemporary and contemptuous criticism of his book: to this we shall return, but anglers, as a rule, unlike Franck, must have been for the king, and on Izaak's side in controversy.

Walton brought out a second edition in 1655. He rewrote the book, adding more than a third, suppressing *Viator*, and introducing *Venator*. New plates were added, and, after the manner of the time, commendatory verses. A third edition appeared in 1661, a fourth (published by Simon Gape, not by Marriott) came out in 1664, a fifth in 1668 (counting Gape's of 1664 as a new edition), and in 1676, the work, with treatises by Venables and Charles Cotton, was given to the world as *The Universal Angler*. Five editions in twelve years is not bad evidence of Walton's popularity. But times now altered. Walton is really an Elizabethan: he has the quaint freshness, the apparently artless music of language of the great age. He is a friend of " country contents ": no lover of the town, no keen student of urban ways and mundane men. A new taste, modelled on that of the wits of Louis XIV., had come in: we are in the period of Dryden, and approaching that of Pope.

There was no new edition of Walton till Moses Browne (by Johnson's desire) published him, with " improvements," in 1750. Then came Hawkins's edition in 1760. Johnson said of Hawkins, " Why, ma'am, I believe him to be an honest man at the bottom; but, to be sure, he is penurious, and he is mean, and it must be owned he has a degree of brutality, and a tendency to savageness, that cannot easily be defended."

This was hardly the editor for Izaak! However, Hawkins, probably by aid of Oldys the antiquary (as Mr. Marston shows), laid a good foundation for a biography of Walton. Errors he made, but Sir Harris Nicolas has corrected them. Johnson himself reckoned Walton's *Lives* as " one of his most favourite books." He preferred the life of Donne, and justly complained that Walton's story of Donne's vision of his absent wife had been left out of a modern edition. He explained Walton's friendship with persons of higher rank by his being "a great panegyrist."

The eighteenth century, we see, came back to Walton, as the nineteenth has done. He was precisely the author to suit Charles Lamb. He was reprinted again and again, and illustrated by Stoddart and others. Among his best editors are Major (1839), "Ephemera" (1853), Nicolas (1836, 1860), and Mr. Marston (1888).

The only contemporary criticism known to me is that of Richard Franck, who had served with Cromwell in Scotland, and, not liking the aspect of changing times, returned to the north, and fished from the Esk to Strathnaver. In 1658 he wrote his *Northern Memoirs*, an itinerary of sport, heavily cumbered by dull reflections and pedantic style. Franck, however, was a practical angler, especially for salmon, a fish of which Walton knew nothing: he also appreciated the character of the great Montrose. He went to America, wrote a wild cosmogonic work, and *The Admirable and Indefatigable Adventures of the Nine Pious Pilgrims* (one pilgrim catches a trout!) (London, 1708). The *Northern Memoirs* of 1658 were not published till 1694. Sir Walter Scott edited a new issue, in 1821, and defended Izaak from the strictures of the salmon-fisher. Izaak, says Franck, "lays the stress of his arguments upon other men's observations, wherewith he stuffs his indigested octavo; so brings himself under the angler's censure and the common calamity of a plagiary, to be pitied (poor man) for his loss of time, in scribbling and transcribing other men's notions. . . . I remember in Stafford, I urged his own argument upon him, that pickerel weed of itself breeds pickerel (pike)." Franck proposed a rational theory, " which my Compleat Angler no sooner deliberated, but dropped his argument, and leaves Gesner to defend it, so huffed away. . . ." " So note, the true character of an industrious angler more deservedly falls upon Merrill and Faulkner, or rather Izaak Ouldham, a man that fished salmon with but three hairs at hook, whose collections and experiments were lost with himself,"—a matter much to be regretted. It will be observed, of course, that hair was then used, and gut is first mentioned for angling purposes by Mr. Pepys. Indeed, the flies which Scott was hunting for when he found the lost MS. of the first part of *Waverley* are tied on horse-hairs. They are in the possession of the descendants of Scott's friend, Mr. William Laidlaw. The curious angler, consulting Franck, will find that his salmon flies are much like our own, but less variegated. Scott justly remarks that, while Walton was by habit and repute a bait-fisher, even Cotton knows nothing of salmon. Scott wished that Walton had made the northern tour, but Izaak would have been sadly to seek, running after a fish down a gorge of the Shin or the Brora, and the discomforts of the north would have finished his career. In Scotland he would not have found fresh sheets smelling of lavender.

Walton was in London "in the dangerous year 1655." He speaks of his meeting Bishop Sanderson there, "in sad-coloured clothes, and, God knows, far from being costly." The friends were driven by wind and rain into "a cleanly house, where we had bread, cheese, ale, and a fire, for our ready money. The rain and wind were so obliging to me, as to force our stay there for at least an hour, to my great content and advantage; for in that time he made to me many useful observations of the present times with much clearness and conscientious freedom." It was a year of Republican and Royalist conspiracies: the clergy were persecuted and banished from London.

No more is known of Walton till the happy year 1660, when the king came to his own again, and Walton's Episcopal friends to their palaces. Izaak produced an " Eglog," on 29th May:

> The king! The king's returned! And now
> Let's banish all sad thoughts, and sing:
> We have our laws, and have our king.

If Izaak was so eccentric as to go to bed sober on that glorious twenty-ninth of May, I greatly misjudge him. But he grew elderly. In 1661 he chronicles the deaths of " honest Nat. and R. Roe, —they are gone, and with them most of my pleasant hours, even as a shadow that passeth away, and returns not." On 17th April, 1662, Walton lost his second wife: she died at Worcester, probably on a visit to Bishop Morley. In the same year, the bishop was translated to Winchester, where the palace became Izaak's home. The Itchen (where, no doubt, he angled with worm) must have been his constant haunt. He was busy with his Life of Richard Hooker (1665). The peroration, as it were, was altered and expanded in 1670, and this is but one example of Walton's care of his periods. One beautiful passage he is known to have rewritten several times, till his ear was satisfied with its cadences. In 1670 he published his Life of George Herbert. " I wish, if God shall be so pleased, that I may be so happy as to die like him." In 1673, in a dedication of the third edition of *Reliquiæ Wottonianæ*, Walton alludes to his friendship with a much younger and gayer man than himself, Charles Cotton (born 1630), the friend of Colonel Richard Lovelace, and of Sir John Suckling: the translator of Scarron's travesty of Virgil, and of Montaigne's *Essays*. Cotton was a roisterer, a man at one time deep in debt, but he was a Royalist, a scholar, and an angler. The friendship between him and Walton is creditable to the freshness of the old man and to the kindness of the younger, who, to be sure, laughed at Izaak's heavily dubbed London flies. " In him," says Cotton, " I have the happiness to know the worthiest man, and to enjoy the best and the truest friend any man ever had." We are reminded of Johnson with Langton and Topham Beauclerk. Meanwhile Izaak the younger had grown up, was educated under Dr. Fell at Christ Church, and made the Grand Tour in 1675, visiting Rome and Venice. In March 1676 he proceeded M.A. and took Holy Orders. In this year Cotton wrote his treatise on fly-fishing, to be published with Walton's new edition; and the famous fishing house on the Dove, with the blended initials of the two friends, was built   In 1678, Walton wrote his Life of Sanderson. . . . " 'Tis now too late to wish that my life may be like his, for I am in the eighty-fifth year of my age, but I humbly beseech Almighty God that my death may be; and do as earnestly beg of every reader to say Amen!" He wrote, in 1678, a preface to *Thealma and Clearchus* (1683). The poem is attributed to John Chalkhill, a Fellow of Winchester College, who died, a man of eighty, in 1679. Two of his songs are in *The Compleat Angler*. Probably the attribution is right: Chalkhill's tomb commemorates a man after Walton's own heart, but some have assigned the volume to Walton himself. Chalkhill is described, on the title-page, as " an acquaintant and friend of Edmund Spencer," which is impossible.[1]

On 9th August, 1683, Walton wrote his will, " in the neintyeth year of my age, and in perfect memory, for which praised be God." He professes the Anglican faith, despite " a very long and very trew friendship for some of the Roman Church." His worldly estate he has acquired " neither by falsehood or flattery or the extreme crewelty of the law of this nation." His property was in two houses in London, the lease of Norington farm, a farm near

---

[1] There is an edition by Singer, with a frontispiece by Wainewright, the poisoner. London, 1820.

Stafford, besides books, linen, and a hanging cabinet inscribed with his name, now, it seems, in the possession of Mr. Elkin Mathews. A bequest is made of money for coals to the poor of Stafford, " every last weike in Janewary, or in every first weike in Febrewary; I say then, because I take that time to be the hardest and most pinching times with pore people." To the Bishop of Winchester he bequeathed a ring with a posy, " A Mite for a Million." There are other bequests, including ten pounds to " my old friend, Mr. Richard Marriott," Walton's bookseller. This good man died in peace with his publisher, leaving him also a ring. A ring was left to a lady of the Portsmouth family, " Mrs. Doro. Wallop."

Walton died, at the house of his son-in-law, Dr. Hawkins, in Winchester, on 15th December, 1683: he is buried in the south aisle of the cathedral. The Cathedral library possesses many of Walton's books, with his name written in them. His *Eusebius* (1636) contains, on the flyleaf, repetitions, in various forms, of one of his studied passages. Simple as he seems, he is a careful artist in language.

Such are the scanty records, and scantier relics, of a very long life. Circumstances and inclination combined to make Walton choose the *fallentis semita vitæ*. Without ambition, save to be in the society of good men, he passed through turmoil, ever companioned by content. For him existence had its trials: he saw all that he held most sacred overthrown; laws broken up; his king publicly

murdered; his friends outcasts; his worship pro-
scribed; he himself suffered in property from the
raid of the Kirk into England. He underwent
many bereavements: child after child he lost, but
content he did not lose, nor sweetness of heart, nor
belief. His was one of those happy characters
which are never found disassociated from unques-
tioning faith. Of old he might have been the
ancient religious Athenian in the opening of Plato's
Republic, or Virgil's aged gardener. The happiness
of such natures would be incomplete without religion, but only by such tranquil and blessed souls
can religion be accepted with no doubt or scruple,
no dread, and no misgiving. In his preface to
Thealma and Clearchus Walton writes, and we may
use his own words about his own works: "The
Reader will here find such various events and rewards
of innocent Truth and undissembled Honesty, as is
like to leave in him (if he be a good-natured reader)
more sympathising and virtuous impressions, than
ten times so much time spent in impertinent, critical
and needless disputes about religion." Walton
relied on authority; on "a plain, unperplexed cate-
chism." In an age of the strangest and most dis-
sident theological speculations, an age of Quakers,
Anabaptists, Antinomians, Fifth Monarchy Men,
Covenanters, Independents, Gibbites, Presbyterians,
and what not, Walton was true to the authority
of the Church of England, with no prejudice
against the ancient Catholic faith. As Gesner
was his authority for pickerel weed begetting

pike, so the Anglican bishops were security for
Walton's creed.

To him, if we may say so, it was easy to be
saved, while Bunyan, a greater humorist, could be
saved only in following a path that skirted madness,
and "as by fire." To Bunyan, Walton would have
seemed a figure like his own Ignorance; a pilgrim
who never stuck in the Slough of Despond, nor
met Apollyon in the Valley of the Shadow, nor
was captive in Doubting Castle, nor stoned in
Vanity Fair. And of Bunyan, Walton would have
said that he was among those Noncomformists who
"might be sincere, well-meaning men, whose indis-
creet zeal might be so like charity, as thereby to
cover a multitude of errors." To Walton there
seemed spiritual solace in remembering "that we
have comforted and been helpful to a dejected or
distressed family." Bunyan would have regarded
this belief as a heresy, and (theoretically) charitable
deeds "as filthy rags." Differently constituted,
these excellent men accepted religion in different
ways. Christian bows beneath a burden of sin;
Piscator beneath a basket of trout. Let us be
grateful for the diversities of human nature, and the
dissimilar paths which lead Piscator and Christian
alike to the City not built with hands. Both were
seekers for a City which to have sought through
life, in patience, honesty, loyalty, and love, is to
have found it. Of Walton's book we may say:

*Laudis amore tumes ? Sunt certa piacula quæ te
Ter pure lecto poterunt recreare libello.*

Franck, as we saw, called Walton "a plagiary." He was a plagiary in the same sense as Virgil and Lord Tennyson and Robert Burns, and, indeed, Homer, and all poets. *The Compleat Angler*, the father of so many books, is the child of a few. Walton not only adopted the opinions and advice of the authors whom he cites, but also follows the manner, to a certain extent, of authors whom he does not quote. His very exordium, his key-note, echoes (as Sir Harris Nicolas observes) the opening of *A Treatise of the Nature of God* (London, 1599). The *Treatise* starts with a conversation between a gentleman and a scholar; it commences:

> *Gent.* Well overtaken, sir!
> *Scholar.* You are welcome, gentleman.

A more important source is *The Treatyse of Fysshynge wyth an Angle*, commonly attributed to Dame Juliana Barnes (printed at Westminster, 1496). A manuscript, probably of 1430-1450, has been published by Mr. Satchell (London, 1883). This book may be a translation of an unknown French original. It opens:

Soloman in hys paraboles seith that a glad spirit maket a flowryng age. That ys to sey, a feyre age and a longe [like Walton's own], and sith hyt ys so I aske this question, wyche bynne the menys and cause to reduce a man to a mery spryte. The angler schall have hys holsom walke and mery at hys owne ease, and also many a sweyt eayr of divers erbis and flowres that schall make hym ryght hongre and well disposed in hys body. He schall heyr the melodies melodious of the ermony of byrde: he schall se also the yong swannes and signetes folowing ther eyrours, duckes, cootes, herons, and many other fowlys with ther brodys, wyche me semyt better then all the noyse of houndes, and blastes of hornes and other gamys that fawkners or hunters can make, and yf the angler take the fyssche, hardly then ys ther no man meryer then he in his sprites.

This is the very "sprite" of Walton; this has that vernal and matutinal air of opening European literature, full of birds' music, and redolent of dawn. This is the note to which the age following Walton would not listen.

In matter of fact, again, Izaak follows the ancient *Treatise*. We know his jury of twelve flies; the *Treatise* says:

These ben the xij flyes wyth whyche ye shall angle to the trought and graylling, and dubbe like as ye shall now here me tell.
Marche. The donne fly, the body of the donne woll, and the wyngis of the pertryche. Another donne flye, the body of blacke woll, the wyngis of the blackyst drake; and the lay under the wynge and under the tayle.

Walton has:

The first is the dun fly in March: the body is made of dun wool, the wings of the partridge's feathers. The second is another dun fly: the body of black wool; and the wings made of the black drake's feathers, and of the feathers under his tail.

Again, the *Treatise* has:

Auguste. The drake fly. The body of black wull and lappyd abowte wythe blacke sylke: winges of the mayle of the blacke drake wyth a blacke heed.

170

Walton has:

The twelfth is the dark drake-fly, good in August: the body made with black wool, lapt about with black silk, his wings are made with the mail of the black drake, with a black head.

This is word for word a transcript of the fifteenth century *Treatise*. But Izaak cites, not the ancient *Treatise*, but Mr. Thomas Barker.[1] Barker, in fact, gives many more, and more variegated flies than Izaak offers in the jury of twelve which he rendered, from the old *Treatise*, into modern English. Sir Harris Nicolas says that the jury is from Leonard Mascall's *Booke of Fishing with Hooke and Line* (London, 1609), but Mascall merely stole from the fifteenth-century book. In Cotton's practice, and that of *The Angler's Vade Mecum* (1681), flies were as numerous as among ourselves, and had, in many cases, the same names. Walton absurdly bids us " let no part of the line touch the water, but the fly only." Barker says, " Let the fly light first into the water." Both men insist on fishing down stream, which is, of course, the opposite of the true art, for fish lie with their heads up stream, and trout are best approached from behind. Cotton admits of fishing both up and down, as the wind and stream may serve: and, of course, in heavy water, in Scotland, this is all very well. But none of the old anglers, to my knowledge, was a dry-fly fisher, and Izaak was no fly-fisher at all. He took what

---

[1] *Barker's Delight ; or, The Art of Angling.* 1651, 1657, 1659, London.

he said from Mascall, who took it from the old *Treatise*, in which, it is probable, Walton read, and followed the pleasant and to him congenial spirit of the mediæval angler. All these writers tooled with huge rods, fifteen or eighteen feet in length, and Izaak had apparently never used a reel. For salmon, he says, "some use a wheel about the middle of their rods or near their hand, which is to be observed better by seeing one of them, than by a large demonstration of words."

Mr. Westwood has made a catalogue of books cited by Walton in his *Compleat Angler*. There is Ælian (who makes the first known reference to fly-fishing); Aldrovandus, *De Piscibus* (1638); Dubravius, *De Piscibus* (1559); and the English translation (1599); Gerard's *Herball* (1633); Gesner, *De Piscibus (s.a.)* and *Historia Naturalis* (1558); Phil. Holland's *Pliny* (1601); Rondelet, *De Piscibus Marinis* (1554); Silvianus, *Aquatilium Historiæ* (1554): these nearly exhaust Walton's supply of authorities in natural history. He was devoted, as we saw, to authority, and had a childlike faith in the fantastic theories which date from Pliny. "Pliny hath an opinion that many flies have their birth, or being, from a dew that in the spring falls upon the leaves of trees." It is a pious opinion! Izaak is hardly so superstitious as the author of *The Angler's Vade Mecum*. I cannot imagine him taking "Man's fat and cat's fat, of each half an ounce, mummy finely powdered, three drams," and a number of other abominations, to "make an Oyntment according to Art, and when you Angle, anoint 8 inches of the line next the Hook therewith." Or, "Take the Bones and Scull of a Dead-man, at the opening of a Grave, and beat the same into Pouder, and put of this Pouder in the Moss wherein you keep your Worms,—*but others like Grave Earth as well.*" No doubt grave earth is quite as efficacious.

These remarks show how Izaak was equipped in books and in practical information; it follows that his book is to be read, not for instruction, but for human pleasure.

So much for what Walton owed to others. For all the rest, for what has made him the favourite of schoolboys and sages, of poets and philosophers, he is indebted to none but his Maker and his genius. That he was a lover of Montaigne we know; and, had Montaigne been a fisher, he might have written somewhat like Izaak, but without the piety, the perfume, and the charm. There are authors whose living voices, if we know them in the flesh, we seem to hear in our ears as we peruse their works. Of such was Mr. Jowett, sometime Master of Balliol College, a good man, now with God. It has ever seemed to me that friends of Walton must thus have heard his voice as they read him, and that it reaches us too, though faintly. Indeed, we have here "a kind of picture of his own disposition," as he tells us Piscator is the Walton whom honest Nat. and R. Roe and Sir Henry Wotton knew on fishing-days. The book is a set of confessions, without their commonly morbid turn. "I write

not for money, but for pleasure," he says; methinks
he drove no hard bargain with good Richard
Marriott, nor was careful and troubled about
royalties on his eighteenpenny book. He regards
scoffers as " an abomination to mankind," for indeed
even Dr. Johnson, who, a century later, set Moses
Browne on reprinting *The Compleat Angler*, broke
his jest on our suffering tribe. " Many grave,
serious men pity anglers," says Auceps, and Venator
styles them " patient men," as surely they have
great need to be. For our toil, like that of the
husbandman, hangs on the weather that Heaven
sends, and on the flies that have their birth or being
from a kind of dew, and on the inscrutable caprice
of fish; also, in England, on the miller, who giveth
or withholdeth at his pleasure the very water that
is our element. The inquiring rustic who shambles
up erect when we are lying low among the reeds,
even he disposes of our fortunes, with whom, as
with all men, we must be patient, dwelling ever

> With close-lipped Patience for our only friend,
> Sad Patience, too near neighbour of Despair.

O the tangles, more than Gordian, of gut on a
windy day! O bitter east wind that bloweth down
stream! O the young ducks that, swimming between us and the trout, contend with him for the
blue duns in their season! O the hay grass behind
us that entangles the hook! O the rocky wall that
breaks it, the boughs that catch it; the drought
that leaves the salmon-stream dry, the floods that

fill it with turbid, impossible waters! Alas for the
knot that breaks, and for the iron that bends; for
the lost landing-net, and the gillie with the gaff
that scrapes the fish! Izaak believed that fish
could hear; if they can, their vocabulary must be
full of strange oaths, for all anglers are not patient
men. A malison on the trout that "bulge" and
"tail," on the salmon that "jiggers," or sulks, or
lightly gambols over and under the line. These
things, and many more, we anglers endure meekly,
being patient men, and a light world fleers at us
for our very virtue.

Izaak, of course, justifies us by the example of
the primitive Christians, and, in the manner of the
age, drowns opposition in a flood of erudition, out
of place, but never pedantic; futile, yet diverting;
erroneous, but not dull.

"God is said to have spoken to a fish, but never
to a beast." There is a modern Greek phrase, "By
the first word of God, and the second of the fish."
As for angling, "it is somewhat like poetry: men
are to be born so"; and many are born to be both
rhymers and anglers. But, unlike many poets, the
angler resembles "the Adonis, or Darling of the
Sea, so called because it is a loving and innocent
fish," and a peaceful; "and truly, I think most
anglers are so disposed to most of mankind."

Our Saviour's peculiar affection for fishermen is,
of course, a powerful argument. And it is certain
that Peter, James, and John made converts among
the twelve, for "the greater number of them were

found together, fishing, by Jesus after His Resurrection." That Amos was "a good-natured, plain fisherman," only Walton had faith enough to believe. He fixes gladly on mentions of hooks in the Bible, omitting Homer, and that excellent Theocritean dialogue of the two old anglers and the fish of gold, which would have delighted Izaak, had he known it; but he was no great scholar. "And let me tell you that in the Scripture, angling is always taken in the best sense," though Izaak does not dwell on Tobias's enormous capture. So he ends with commendations of angling by Wotton, and Davors (Dennys, more probably), author of *The Secrets of Angling* (1613). To these we may add Wordsworth, Thomson, Scott, Hogg, Stoddart, and many minor poets who loved the music of the reel.

Izaak next illustrates his idea of becoming mirth, which excludes "Scripture jests and lascivious jests," both of them highly distasteful to anglers. Then he comes to practice, beginning with chub, for which I have never angled, but have taken them by misadventure, with a salmon fly. Thence we proceed to trout, and to the charming scene of the milkmaid and her songs by Raleigh and Marlowe, "I think much better than the strong lines that are now in fashion in this critical age," for Walton, we have said, was the last of the Elizabethans, and the new times were all for Waller and Dryden. "Chevy Chace" and "Johnny Armstrong" were dear to Walton as to Scott, but through a century these old favourites were to be neglected, save by Mr.

Pepys and Addison. Indeed, there is no more curious proof of the great unhappy change then coming to make poetry a mechanic art, than the circumstance that Walton is much nearer to us, in his likings, than to the men between 1670 and 1770. Gay was to sing of angling, but in " the strong lines that are now in fashion." All this while Piscator has been angling with worm and minnow to no purpose, though he picks up " a trout will fill six reasonable bellies " in the evening. So we leave them after their ale, " in fresh sheets that smell of lavender." Izaak's practical advice is not of much worth; we read him rather for sentences like this: " I'll tell you, scholar: when I sat last on this primrose bank, and looked down these meadows, I thought of them as Charles the Emperor did of the city of Florence, ' that they were too pleasant to be looked upon, but only on holy-days.' " He did not say, like Fox, when Burke spoke of " a seat under a tree, with a friend, a bottle, and a book," " Why a book ? " Izaak took his book with him— a practice in which, at least, I am fain to imitate this excellent old man.

As to salmon, Walton scarcely speaks a true word about their habits, except by accident. Concerning pike, he quotes the theory that they are bred by pickerel weed, only as what " some think." In describing the use of frogs as bait, he makes the famous, or infamous, remark, " Use him as though you loved him . . . that he may live the longer." A bait-fisher *may* be a good man, as Izaak was, but

it is easier for a camel to pass through the eye of a
needle. As coarse fish are usually caught only with
bait, I shall not follow Izaak on to this unholy and
unfamiliar ground, wherein, none the less, grow
flowers of Walton's fancy, and the songs of the old
poets are heard. *The Compleat Angler*, indeed, is a
book to be marked with flowers, marsh-marigolds
and fritillaries, and petals of the yellow iris, for the
whole provokes us to content, and whispers that
word of the apostle, " Study to be quiet."

Since Maui, the Maori hero, invented barbs for
hooks, angling has been essentially one and the
same thing. South Sea islanders spin for fish with
a mother-of-pearl lure which is also a hook, and
answers to our spoon. We have hooks of stone,
and hooks of bone; and a bronze hook, found in
Ireland, has the familiar Limerick bend. What
Homer meant by making anglers throw " the horn
of an ox of the stall " into the sea, we can only
guess; perhaps a horn minnow is meant, or a little
sheath of horn to protect the line. Dead bait, live
bait, and imitations of bait have all been employed,
and Ælian mentions artificial Mayflies used, with
a very short line, by the Illyrians.

But, while the same in essence, angling has been
improved by human ingenuity. The Waltonian
angler, and still more his English predecessors,
dealt much in the home-made. The *Treatise* of
the fifteenth century bids you make your " Rodde "
of a fair staff even of a six foot long or more, as ye

list, of hazel, willow, or "aspe" (ash ?), and "beke hym in an ovyn when ye bake, and let him cool and dry a four weeks or more." The pith is taken out of him with a hot iron, and a yard of white hazel is similarly treated, also a fair shoot of blackthorn or crabtree for a top. The butt is bound with hoops of iron, the top is accommodated with a noose, a hair line is looped in the noose, and the angler is equipped. Splicing is not used, but the joints have holes to receive each other, and with this instrument "ye may walk, and there is no man shall wit whereabout ye go." Recipes are given for colouring and plaiting hair lines, and directions for forging hooks. "The smallest quarell needles" are used for the tiniest hooks.

Barker (1651) makes the rod "of a hasel of one piece, or of two pieces set together in the most convenient manner, light and gentle." He recommends the use of a single hair next the fly,—"you shall have more rises," which is true, "and kill more fish," which is not so likely. The most delicate striking is required with fine gut, and with a single hair there must be many breakages. For salmon, Barker uses a rod ten feet in the butt, "that will carry a top of six foot pretty stiffe and strong." The "winder," or reel, Barker illustrates with a totally unintelligible design. His salmon fly "carries six wings"; perhaps he only means wings composed of six kinds of feathers, but here Franck is a better authority, his flies being sensible and sober in colour. Not many old salmon flies are in existence, nor have I seen more ancient specimens than a few, chiefly of peacocks' feathers, in the fly-leaf of a book at Abbotsford; they were used in Ireland by Sir Walter Scott's eldest son. The controversy as to whether fish can distinguish colours was unknown to our ancestors. I am inclined to believe that, for salmon, size, and perhaps shade, light or dark, with more or less of tinsel, are the only important points. Izaak stumbled on the idea of Mr. Stewart (author of *The Practical Angler*) saying, " for the generality, three or four flies, neat, and rightly made, and not too big, serve for a trout in most rivers, all the summer." Our ancestors, though they did not fish with the dry fly, were intent on imitating the insect on the water. As far as my own experience goes, if trout are feeding on duns, one dun will take them as well as another, if it be properly presented. But my friend Mr. Charles Longman tells me that, after failing with two trout, he examined the fly on the water, an olive dun, and found in his book a fly which exactly matched the natural insect in colour. With this he captured his brace.

Such incidents look as if trout were particular to a shade, but we can never be certain that the angler did not make an especially artful and delicate cast when he succeeded. Sir Herbert Maxwell intends to make the experiment of using duns of impossible and unnatural colours; if he succeeds with these, on several occasions, as well as with orthodox flies, perhaps we may decide that trout do not distinguish hues. On a Sutherland loch, an angler found that trout would take flies of any colour, except that of a light-green leaf of a tree. This rejection decidedly looked as if even Sutherland loch trout exercised some discrimination. Often, on a loch, out of three flies they will favour one, and that, perhaps, not the trail fly. The best rule is: when you find a favourite fly on a salmon river, use it: its special favouritism may be a superstition, but, at all events, salmon do take it. We cannot afford to be always making experiments, but Mr. Herbert Spencer, busking his flies the reverse way, used certainly to be at least as successful with sea trout as his less speculative neighbours in Argyllshire.

In making rods, Walton is most concerned with painting them: " I think a good top is worth preserving, or I had not taken care to keep a top above twenty years." Cotton prefers rods " made in Yorkshire," having advanced from the home-made stage. His were spliced, and kept up all through the season, as he had his water at his own door, while Walton trudged to the Lea and other streams near London, when he was not fishing the Itchen, or Shawford Brook. *The Angler's Vade Mecum* recommends eighteen-feet rods: preferring a fir butt, fashioned by the arrow-maker, a hazel top, and a tip of whalebone. This authority, even more than Walton, deals in mysterious " Oyntments " of gum ivy, horse-leek, asafœtida, man's fat, cat's fat, powdered skulls, and grave earth. A ghoulish body is the angler of the *Vade Mecum*. He recommends up-stream fishing, with worm, in a clear water, and so is a predecessor of Mr. Stewart. "When you have hooked a good fish, have an especial care to keep the rod bent, lest he run to the end of the line" (he means, as does Walton, lest he pull the rod horizontal) "and break either hook or hold." An old owner of my copy adds, in manuscript, "And hale him not to near ye top of the water, lest in flaskering he break ye line."

This is a favourite device of sea trout, which are very apt to "flasker" on the top of the water. The *Vade Mecum*, in advance of Walton on this point, recommends a swivel in minnow-fishing: but has no idea of an artificial minnow of silk. I have known an ingenious lady who, when the bodies of her phantom minnows gave out, in Norway, supplied their place successfully with bed-quilting artfully sewn. In fact, anything bright and spinning will allure fish, though in the upper Ettrick, where large trout exist, they will take the natural, but perhaps never the phantom or angel minnow. I once tried a spinning Alexandra fly over some large pond trout. They followed it eagerly, but never took hold, on the first day; afterwards they would not look at it at all. The *Vade Mecum* man, like Dr. Hamilton, recommends a light fly for a light day, a dark fly for a dark day and dark weather; others hold the converse opinion. Every one agrees that the smallness of the flies should be in proportion to the lowness of the water and the advance of summer.

Our ancestors, apparently, used only one fly at a

time; in rapid rivers, with wet fly, two, three, or, in lochs like Loch Leven, even four are employed. To my mind more than two only cause entanglements of the tackle. The old English anglers knew, of course, little or nothing of loch fishing, using bait in lakes. The great length of their rods made reels less necessary, and they do not seem to have waded much. A modern angler, casting upwards, from the middle of the stream, with a nine-foot rod, would have astonished Walton. They dealt with trout less educated than ours, and tooled with much coarser and heavier implements. They had no fine scruples about bait of every kind, any more than the Scots have, and Barker loved a lob-worm, fished on the surface, in a dark night. He was a pot-fisher, and had been a cook. He could catch a huge basket of trout, and dress them in many different ways—"broyled, calvored hot with ant-chovaes sauce, boyled, soused, stewed, fried, battered with eggs, roasted, baked, calvored cold, and marilled, or potted, also marrionated." Barker instructs my Lord Montague to fish with salmon roe, a thing prohibited and very popular in Scotland. "If I had known it but twenty years agoe, I would have gained a hundred pounds onely with that bait. I am bound in duty to divulge it to your Honour, and not to carry it to my grave with me. I do desire that men of quality should have it that delight in that pleasure: the greedy angler will murmur at me, but for that I care not." Barker calls salmon roe "an experience I have found of late: the best bait for a trout that I have seen in all my time," and it *is* the most deadly, in the eddy of a turbid water. Perhaps trout would take caviare, which is not forbidden by the law of the land. Any unscrupulous person may make the experiment, and argue the matter out with the water-bailie. But, in my country, it is more usual to duck that official, and go on netting, sniggling, salmon-roeing, and destroying sport in the sacred name of Liberty.

> Scots wha fish wi' salmon roe,
> Scots wha sniggle as ye go,
> Wull ye stand the Bailie? No!
> Let the limmer die!

> Now's the day and now's the time,
> Poison a' the burns wi' lime,
> Fishing fair's a dastard crime,
> We're for fishing *free*!

" Ydle persones sholde have but lyttyl mesure in the sayd dysporte of fysshyng," says our old *Treatise*, but in southern Scotland they have left few fish to " dysporte " with, and the trout is like to become an extinct animal. Izaak would especially have disliked Fishing Competitions, which, by dint of the multitude of anglers, turn the contemplative man's recreation into a crowded skirmish; and we would repeat his remark, " the rabble herd themselves together " (a dozen in one pool, often), " and endeavour to govern and act in spite of authority."

For my part, had I a river, I would gladly let all honest anglers that use the fly cast line in it, but, where there is no protection, then nets, poison, dynamite, slaughter of fingerlings, and unholy baits devastate the fish, so that " Free Fishing " spells no fishing at all. This presses most hardly on the artisan who fishes fair, a member of a large class with whose pastime only a churl would wish to interfere. We are now compelled, if we would catch fish, to seek tarpon in Florida, mahseer in India; it does not suffice to " stretch our legs up Tottenham Hill."

THE DEATH OF ROBERT LOUIS STEVENSON

By Sir A. T. Quiller-Couch

WHEN the telegram came, early one Monday
morning, what was our first thought, as soon as the
immediate numbness of sorrow passed and the selfish
instinct began to reassert itself (as it always does)
and whisper "What have *I* lost? What is the
difference to *me*?" Was it not something like this
—"Put away books and paper and pen. Stevenson
is dead. Stevenson is dead, and now there is nobody
left to write for." Our children and grandchildren
shall rejoice in his books; but we of this generation
possessed in the living man something that they
will not know. So long as he lived, though it were
far from Britain—though we had never spoken to
him and he, perhaps, had barely heard our names
—we always wrote our best for Stevenson. To
him each writer amongst us—small or more than
small—had been proud to have carried his best.
That best might be poor enough. So long as it
was not slipshod, Stevenson could forgive. While
he lived, he moved men to put their utmost even
into writings that quite certainly would never meet
his eye. Surely another age will wonder over this

curiosity of letters—that for five years the needle of literary endeavour in Great Britain has quivered towards a little island in the South Pacific, as to its magnetic pole.

Yet he founded no school, though most of us from time to time have poorly tried to copy him. He remained altogether inimitable, yet never seemed conscious of his greatness. It was native in him to rejoice in the successes of other men at least as much as in his own triumphs. One almost felt that, so long as good books were written, it was no great concern to him whether he or others wrote them. Born with an artist's craving for beauty of expression, he achieved that beauty with infinite pains. Confident in romance and in the beneficence of joy, he cherished the flame of joyous romance with more than Vestal fervour, and kept it ardent in a body which Nature, unkind from the beginning, seemed to delight in visiting with more unkindness—a " soul's dark cottage, battered and decayed " almost from birth. And his books leave the impression that he did this chiefly from a sense of duty: that he laboured and kept the lamp alight chiefly because, for the time, other and stronger men did not.

Had there been another Scott, another Dumas —if I may change the image—to take up the torch of romance and run with it, I doubt if Stevenson would have offered himself. I almost think in that case he would have consigned with Nature and sat at ease, content to read of new Ivanhoes and new

D'Artagnans: for—let it be said again—no man had less of the ignoble itch for merely personal success. Think, too, of what the struggle meant for him: how it drove him unquiet about the world, if somewhere he might meet with a climate to repair the constant drain upon his feeble vitality; and how at last it flung him, as by a "sudden freshet," upon Samoa—to die "far from Argos, dear land of home."

And then consider the brave spirit that carried him—the last of a great race—along this far and difficult path; for it is the man we must consider now, not, for the moment, his writings. Fielding's voyage to Lisbon was long and tedious enough; but almost the whole of Stevenson's life has been a voyage to Lisbon, a voyage in the very penumbra of death. Yet Stevenson spoke always as gallantly as his great predecessor. Their "cheerful stoicism," which allies his books with the best British breeding, will keep them classical as long as our nation shall value breeding. It shines to our dim eyes now, as we turn over the familiar pages of *Virginibus Puerisque*, and from page after page—in sentences and fragments of sentences—"It is not altogether ill with the invalid after all." . . . "Who would project a serial novel after Thackeray and Dickens had each fallen in mid-course?" [*He* had two books at least in hand and uncompleted, the papers say.] "Who would find heart enough to begin to live, if he dallied with the consideration of death?" . . "What sorry and pitiful quibbling

all this is!" . . . "It is better to live and be done
with it, than to die daily in the sick-room. By all
means begin your folio; even if the doctor does
not give you a year, even if he hesitates over a
month, make one brave push and see what can
be accomplished in a week. . . . For surely, at
whatever age it overtake the man, this is to die
young. . . . The noise of the mallet and chisel
is scarcely quenched, the trumpets are hardly done
blowing, when, trailing with him clouds of glory,
this happy-starred, full-blooded spirit shoots into
the spiritual land."

As it was in *Virginibus Puerisque*, so is it in the
last essay in his last book of essays:

And the Kingdom of Heaven is of the childlike,
of those who are easy to please, who love and who
give pleasure. Mighty men of their hands, the smiters,
and the builders, and the judges, have lived long
and done sternly, and yet preserved this lovely
character: and among our carpet interests and two-
penny concerns, the shame were indelible if *we* should
lose it. *Gentleness and cheerfulness, these come before
all morality ; they are the perfect duties. . . .*

I remember now (as one remembers little things
at such times) that, when first I heard of his going
to Samoa, there came into my head (Heaven knows
why) a trivial, almost ludicrous passage from his
favourite, Sir Thomas Browne: a passage beginning
"He was fruitlessly put in hope of advantage by
change of Air, and imbibing the pure Aërial Nitre
of those Parts; and therefore, being so far spent,
he quickly found Sardinia in Tivoli, and the most

healthful air of little effect, where Death had set her Broad Arrow. . . ." A statelier sentence of the same author occurs to me now: "To live indeed, is to be again ourselves, which being not only a hope, but an evidence in noble believers, it is all one to lie in St. Innocent's Churchyard, as in the sands of Egypt. Ready to be anything in the ecstasy of being ever, and as content with six foot as the *moles* of Adrianus."

This one lies, we are told, on a mountain-top, overlooking the Pacific. At first it seemed so much easier to distrust a News Agency than to accept Stevenson's loss. "O captain, my captain!" . . . One needs not be an excellent writer to feel that writing will be thankless work, now that Stevenson is gone. But the papers by this time leave no room for doubt. "A grave was dug on the summit of Mount Vaea, 1,300 feet above the sea. The coffin was carried up the hill by Samoans with great difficulty, a track having to be cut through the thick bush which covers the side of the hill from the base to the peak." For the good of man, his father and grandfather planted the high sea-lights upon the Inchcape and the Tyree Coast. He, the last of their line, nursed another light and tended it. Their lamps still shine upon the Bell Rock and the Skerryvore; and—though in alien seas, upon a rock of exile—this other light shall continue, unquenchable by age, beneficent, serene.

IRISH FOLK AND FAIRY TALES

By William Butler Yeats

Dr. Corbett, Bishop of Oxford and Norwich, lamented long ago the departure of the English fairies. "In Queen Mary's time," he wrote,

> When Tom came home from labour,
>   Or Cis to milking rose,
> Then merrily, merrily went their tabor,
>   And merrily went their toes.

But now, in the times of James, they had all gone, for "they were of the old profession," and "their songs were Ave Maries." In Ireland they are still extant, giving gifts to the kindly, and plaguing the surly. "Have you ever seen a fairy or such like?" I asked an old man in County Sligo. "Amn't I annoyed with them," was the answer. "Do the fishermen along here know anything of the mermaids?" I asked a woman of a village in County Dublin. "Indeed, they don't like to see them at all," she answered, "for they always bring bad weather." "Here is a man who believes in ghosts," said a foreign sea-captain, pointing to a pilot of my acquaintance. "In every house over there," said the pilot, pointing to his native village of Rosses, "there are several." Certainly that now

old and much respected dogmatist, the Spirit of
the Age, has in no manner made his voice heard
down there. In a little while, for he has gotten a
consumptive appearance of late, he will be covered
over decently in his grave, and another will grow,
old and much respected, in his place, and never be
heard of down there, and after him another and
another and another. Indeed, it is a question whether
any of these personages will ever be heard of outside the newspaper offices and lecture-rooms and
drawing-rooms and eel-pie houses of the cities, or
if the Spirit of the Age is at any time more than a
froth. At any rate, whole troops of their like will
not change the Celt much. Giraldus Cambrensis
found the people of the western islands a trifle
paganish. "How many gods are there?" asked a
priest, a little while ago, of a man from the Island
of Innistor. "There is one on Innistor; but this
seems a big place," said the man, and the priest
held up his hands in horror, as Giraldus had,
just seven centuries before. Remember, I am not
blaming the man; it is very much better to believe
in a number of gods than in none at all, or to think
there is only one, but that he is a little sentimental
and impracticable, and not constructed for the
nineteenth century. The Celt, and his cromlechs,
and his pillar-stones, these will not change much
—indeed, it is doubtful if anybody at all changes
at any time. In spite of hosts of deniers, and asserters,
and wise-men, and professors, the majority still are
averse to sitting down to dine thirteen at table,

or being helped to salt, or walking under a ladder, or seeing a single magpie flirting his chequered tail. There are, of course, children of light who have set their faces against all this, though even a newspaper man, if you entice him into a cemetery at midnight, will believe in phantoms, for every one is a visionary, if you scratch him deep enough. But the Celt is a visionary without scratching.

Yet, be it noticed, if you are a stranger, you will not readily get ghost and fairy legends, even in a western village. You must go adroitly to work, and make friends with the children, and the old men, with those who have not felt the pressure of mere daylight existence, and those with whom it is growing less, and will have altogether taken itself off one of these days. The old women are most learned, but will not so readily be got to talk, for the fairies are very secretive, and much resent being talked of; and are there not many stories of old women who were nearly pinched into their graves or numbed with fairy blasts?

At sea, when the nets are out and the pipes are lit, then will some ancient hoarder of tales become loquacious, telling his histories to the tune of the creaking of the boats. Holy-eve night, too, is a great time, and in old days many tales were to be heard at wakes. But the priests have set faces against wakes.

In the *Parochial Survey of Ireland* it is recorded how the story-tellers used to gather together of an evening, and if any had a different version from the others, they would all recite theirs and vote, and the man who had varied would have to abide by their verdict. In this way stories have been handed down with such accuracy, that the long tale of Deirdre was, in the earlier decades of this century, told almost word for word, as in the very ancient MSS. in the Royal Dublin Society. In one case only it varied, and then the MS. was obviously wrong—a passage had been forgotten by the copyist. But this accuracy is rather in the folk and bardic tales than in the fairy legends, for these vary widely, being usually adapted to some neighbouring village or local fairy-seeing celebrity. Each county has usually some family, or personage, supposed to have been favoured, or plagued, especially by the phantoms, as the Hackets of Castle Hacket, Galway, who had for their ancestor a fairy, or John-o'-Daly of Lisadell, Sligo, who wrote *Eilleen Aroon*, the song the Scotch have stolen and called *Robin Adair*, and which Handel would sooner have written than all his oratorios,[1] and the *O'Donahue of Kerry*. Round these men stories tended to group themselves, sometimes deserting more ancient heroes for the purpose. Round poets have they gathered especially, for poetry in Ireland has always been mysteriously connected with magic.

These folk-tales are full of simplicity and musical occurrences, for they are the literature of a class for whom every incident in the old rut of birth, love, pain, and death has cropped up unchanged for

[1] He lived some time in Dublin, and heard it then.

centuries: who have steeped everything in the heart: to whom everything is a symbol. They have the spade over which man has leant from the beginning. The people of the cities have the machine, which is prose and a *parvenu*. They have few events. They can turn over the incidents of a long life as they sit by the fire. With us nothing has time to gather meaning, and too many things are occurring for even a big heart to hold. It is said the most eloquent people in the world are the Arabs, who have only the bare earth of the desert and a sky swept bare by the sun. "Wisdom has alighted upon three things," goes their proverb: "the hand of the Chinese, the brain of the Frank, and the tongue of the Arab." This, I take it, is the meaning of that simplicity sought for so much in these days by all the poets, and not to be had at any price.

The most notable and typical story-teller of my acquaintance is one Paddy Flynn, a little, bright-eyed, old man, living in a leaky one-roomed cottage of the village of B——, "the most gentle—*i.e.*, fairy—place in the whole of the County Sligo," he says, though others claim that honour for Drumahair or for Drumcliff. A very pious old man, too! You may have some time to inspect his strange figure and ragged hair, if he happen to be in a devout humour, before he comes to the doings of the gentry. A strange devotion! Old tales of Columkill, and what he said to his mother. "How are you to-day, mother?" "Worse!" "May you be worse to-morrow"; and on the next day,

"How are you to-day, mother?" "Worse!" "May you be worse to-morrow"; and on the next, "How are you to-day, mother?" "Better, thank God." "May you be better to-morrow." In which undutiful manner he will tell you Columkill inculcated cheerfulness. Then most likely he will wander off into his favourite theme—how the Judge smiles alike in rewarding the good and condemning the lost to unceasing flames. Very consoling does it appear to Paddy Flynn, this melancholy and apocalyptic cheerfulness of the Judge. Nor seems his own cheerfulness quite earthly—though a very palpable cheerfulness. The first time I saw him he was cooking mushrooms for himself; the next time he was asleep under a hedge, smiling in his sleep. Assuredly some joy not quite of this steadfast earth lightens in those eyes—swift as the eyes of a rabbit—among so many wrinkles, for Paddy Flynn is very old. A melancholy there is in the midst of their cheerfulness—a melancholy that is almost a portion of their joy, the visionary melancholy of purely instinctive natures and of all animals. In the triple solitude of age and eccentricity and partial deafness he goes about much pestered by children.

As to the reality of his fairy and spirit-seeing powers, not all are agreed. One day we were talking of the Banshee. "I have seen it," he said, "down there by the water 'batting' the river with its hands." He it was who said the fairies annoyed him.

Not that the Sceptic is entirely afar even from

these western villages. I found him one morning
as he bound his corn in a merest pocket-handker-
chief of a field. Very different from Paddy Flynn
—Scepticism in every wrinkle of his face, and a
travelled man, too!—a foot-long Mohawk Indian
tattooed on one of his arms to evidence the matter.
"They who travel," says a neighbouring priest,
shaking his head over him, and quoting Thomas
à Kempis, "seldom come home holy." I had
mentioned ghosts to this Sceptic. "Ghosts," said
he; "there are no such things at all, at all, but
the gentry, they stand to reason; for the devil,
when he fell out of heaven, took the weak-minded
ones with him, and they were put into the waste
places. And that's what the gentry are. But they
are getting scarce now, because their time's over,
ye see, and they're going back. But ghosts, no!
And I'll tell ye something more I don't believe
in—the fire of hell"; then, in a low voice, "that's
only invented to give the priests and the parsons
something to do." Thereupon this man, so full
of enlightenment, returned to his corn-binding.

The various collectors of Irish folk-lore have,
from our point of view, one great merit, and from
the point of view of others, one great fault. They
have made their work literature rather than science,
and told us of the Irish peasantry rather than of the
primitive religion of mankind, or whatever else
the folk-lorists are on the gad after. To be considered scientists they should have tabulated all
their tales in forms like grocers' bills—item the

fairy king, item the queen. Instead of this they have caught the very voice of the people, the very pulse of life, each giving what was most noticed in his day. Croker and Lover, full of the ideas of harum-scarum Irish gentility, saw everything humorised. The impulse of the Irish literature of their time came from a class that did not—mainly for political reasons—take the populace seriously, and imagined the country as a humorist's Arcadia; its passion, its gloom, its tragedy, they knew nothing of. What they did was not wholly false; they merely magnified an irresponsible type, found oftenest among boatmen, carmen, and gentlemen's servants, into the type of a whole nation, and created the stage Irishman. The writers of 'Forty-eight, and the famine combined, burst their bubble. Their work had the dash as well as the shallowness of an ascendant and idle class, and in Croker is touched everywhere with beauty—a gentle Arcadian beauty. Carleton, a peasant born, has in many of his stories—more especially in his ghost stories, a much more serious way with him, for all his humour. Kennedy, an old bookseller in Dublin, who seems to have had a something of genuine belief in the fairies, came next in time. He has far less literary faculty, but is wonderfully accurate, giving often the very words the stories were told in. But the best book since Croker is Lady Wilde's *Ancient Legends*. The humour has all given way to pathos and tenderness. We have here the innermost heart of the Celt in the moments he has grown

to love through years of persecution, when, cushion-
ing himself about with dreams, and hearing fairy-
songs in the twilight, he ponders on the soul and
on the dead. Here is the Celt, only it is the
Celt dreaming.

Besides these are two writers of importance,
who have published, so far, nothing in book shape
—Miss Letitia Maclintock and Mr. Douglas
Hyde. Miss Maclintock writes accurately and
beautifully the half Scotch dialect of Ulster; and
Mr. Douglas Hyde has collected a volume of
folk tales in Gaelic, having taken them down, for
the most part, word for word among the Gaelic
speakers of Roscommon and Galway. He is,
perhaps, most to be trusted of all. He knows the
people thoroughly. Others see a phase of Irish life;
he understands all its elements. His work is neither
humorous nor mournful; it is simply life. I hope
he may put some of his gatherings into ballads, for
he is the last of our ballad-writers of the school
of Walsh and Callanan—men whose work seems
fragrant with turf smoke. And this brings to mind
the chap-books. They are to be found brown with
turf smoke on cottage shelves, and are, or were,
sold on every hand by the pedlars, but cannot be
found in any library of this city of the Sassanach.
The Royal Fairy Tales, The Hibernian Tales, and
The Legends of the Fairies are the fairy literature
of the people. It is more like the fairy poetry of
Scotland than of England. The personages of
English fairy literature are merely, in most cases,

mortals beautifully masquerading. Nobody ever
believed in such fairies. They are romantic bubbles
from Provence. Nobody ever laid new milk on
their doorstep for them.

As to my own book, I tried to make it representative of Irish Folk and Fairy Tales, of every
kind of Irish folk-faith. The reader will perhaps wonder that I have not rationalised a single
hob-goblin. I seek for shelter to the words of
Socrates.

"*Phædrus.* I should like to know, Socrates,
whether the place is not somewhere here at which
Boreas is said to have carried off Orithyia from the
banks of the Ilissus?

"*Socrates.* That is the tradition.

"*Phædrus.* And is this the exact spot? The
little stream is delightfully clear and bright; I can
fancy that there might be maidens playing near.

"*Socrates.* I believe the spot is not exactly here,
but about a quarter of a mile lower down, where
you cross to the temple of Artemis, and I think
that there is some sort of an altar of Boreas at
the place.

"*Phædrus.* I do not recollect; but I beseech
you to tell me, Socrates, do you believe this tale?

"*Socrates.* The wise are doubtful, and I should
not be singular if, like them, I also doubted. I
might have a rational explanation that Orithyia
was playing with Pharmacia, when a northern
gust carried her over the neighbouring rocks; and

this being the manner of her death, she was said
to have been carried away by Boreas. There is a
discrepancy, however, about the locality. According
to another version of the story, she was taken from
the Areopagus, and not from this place. Now I
quite acknowledge that these allegories are very
nice, but he is not to be envied who has to invent
them; much labour and ingenuity will be required
of him; and when he has once begun, he must go
on and rehabilitate centaurs and chimeras dire.
Gorgons and winged steeds flow in apace, and
numberless other inconceivable and portentous
monsters. And if he is sceptical about them, and
would fain reduce them one after another to the
rules of probability, this sort of crude philosophy
will take up all his time. Now, I have certainly
not time for such inquiries. Shall I tell you why?
I must first know myself, as the Delphian in-
scription says; to be curious about that which is
not my business, while I am still in ignorance of
my own self, would be ridiculous. And, therefore,
I say farewell to all this; the common opinion is
enough for me. For, as I was saying, I want to
know not about this, but about myself. Am I,
indeed, a wonder more complicated and swollen
with passion than the serpent Typho, or a creature
of gentler and simpler sort, to whom nature has
given a diviner and lowlier destiny?"

THE AUTHOR OF "PETER WILKINS"

BY ARTHUR HENRY BULLEN

IN one of those bright racy essays at which modern
dullness delights to sneer, Hazlitt discussed the
question whether the desire of posthumous fame
is a legitimate aspiration; and the conclusion at
which he arrived was that there is "something of
egotism and even of pedantry in this sentiment."
It is a true saying in literature as in morality that
"he that seeketh his life shall lose it." The world
cares most for those who have cared least for the
world's applause. A nameless minstrel of the North
Country sings a ballad that shall stir men's hearts
from age to age with haunting melody; Southey,
toiling at his epics, is excluded from Parnassus.
Some there are who have knocked at the door of
the Temple of Fame, and have been admitted at
once and for ever. When Thucydides announced
that he intended his history to be a "possession
for all time," there was no mistaking the tone of
authority. But to be enthroned in state, to receive
the homage of the admiring multitude, and then to
be rejected as a pretender,—that is indeed a sorry
fate, and one that may well make us pause before
envying literary despots their titles. The more

closely a writer shrouds himself from view, the more eager are his readers to get a sight of him. The loss of an arm or a leg would be a slight price for a genuine student to pay if only he could discover one new fact about Shakespeare's history. I will not attempt to impose on the reader's credulity by confessing myself eager to acquire information about the author of *Peter Wilkins* at such a sacrifice; but it would have been a sincere pleasure to me if I could have brought to light some particulars about one whose personality must have possessed a more than ordinary charm.

The delightful *voyage imaginaire* here presented to the reader was first published in 1751. An edition appeared immediately afterwards at Dublin; so the book must have had some sale. The introduction and the dedication to the Countess of Northumberland (to whom it will be remembered Percy dedicated his *Reliques* and Goldsmith the first printed copy of his *Edwin and Angelina*) are signed with the initials " R. P."; and for many years the author's full name was unknown. In 1835, Nicol, the printer, sold by auction a number of books and manuscripts in his possession, which had once belonged to Dodsley, the publisher; and when these were being catalogued, the original agreement for the sale of the MS. of *Peter Wilkins* was brought to light. From this document it appeared that the author was Robert Paltock of Clement's Inn, and that he received for the copyright £20, twelve copies of the book, and " the cuts of the first impression " (proof impressions of the illustrations). The writer's name shows him to have been, like his hero, of Cornish origin; but the authors of the admirable and exhaustive *Bibliotheca Cornubiensis* could discover nothing about him beyond the fact that he was not a bencher of Clement's Inn. That Paltock should have chosen Clement's Inn as a place of residence is not surprising. It still keeps something of its ancient repose. The sun-dial is still supported by the negro ;[1] the grass has not lost its freshness, and on August evenings the plane-trees' leaves glint golden in the sun. One may still hear the chimes at midnight as Falstaff and Justice Shallow heard them of old. Here, where only a muffled murmur comes from the work-a-day world, a man in the last century might have dreamed away his life, lonely as Peter Wilkins on the island. One can imagine the amiable recluse composing his homely romance amid such surroundings. Perhaps it was the one labour of his life. He may have come to the Inn originally with the aspiration of making fame and money; and then the spirit of cloistered calm turned him from such vulgar paths, and instead of losing his fine feelings and swelling the ranks of the plutocrats, he gave us a charming romance for our fireside. With the literary men of his day he seems to

[1] The eighteenth-century leaden figure of the negro with his sun-dial was afterwards presented to the Honourable Society of the Inner Temple, in whose Gardens, on the Terrace facing the Thames Embankment, it has been placed.

have had no intercourse. Not a single mention of him is to be found among his contemporaries, and we may be sure that he cut no brilliant figure at the club-houses. No chorus of reviewers chimed the praises of *Peter Wilkins*. So far as I can discover, the *Monthly Review* was the only journal in which the book was noticed, and such criticism as the following can hardly be termed laudatory: " Here is a very strange performance indeed. It seems to be the illegitimate offspring of no very natural conjunction, like *Gulliver's Travels* and *Robinson Crusoe*; but much inferior to the manner of these two performances as to entertainment or utility. It has all that is impossible in the one or improbable in the other, without the wit and spirit of the first, or the just strokes of nature and useful lessons of morality in the second. However, if the invention of wings for mankind to fly with is sufficient amends for all the dullness and unmeaning extravagance of the author, we are willing to allow that his book has some merit, and that he deserves some encouragement at least as an able mechanic, if not as a good author." But the book was not forgotten. A new edition appeared in 1783, and again in the following year. It was included in Weber's " Popular Romances," 1812, and published separately, with some charming plates by Stothard, in 1816. Within the last fifty years it has been frequently issued, entire or mutilated, in a popular form. A drama founded on the romance was acted at Covent Garden on April 16, 1827;

and more than once of late years *Peter Wilkins* has afforded material for pantomimes. In 1763 a French translation (by Philippe Florent de Puisieux) appeared under the title of *Les Hommes Volants, ou les Aventures de Pierre Wilkins*, which was included in vols. xxii.-xxiii. of De Perthe's *Voyages Imaginaires* (1788-89). A German translation was published in 1767, having for title *Die fliegenden Menschen, oder wunderbare Begebenheiten Peter Wilkins*. Whether the author lived to see the translations of this work cannot be ascertained. A Robert Paltock[1] was buried at Ryme Intrinseca Church, Dorset, in 1767, aged seventy (Hutchin's *Dorset*, iv. 493-494, third edition), but it is very doubtful whether he was the author of the romance.

Paltock's fame may be said to be firmly established. An American writer, it is true, in a recent *History of Fiction*, says not a word about *Peter Wilkins*; but, we must remember, another American wrote a *History of Caricature* without mentioning Rowlandson. Coleridge admired the book, and is reported to have said : " *Peter Wilkins* is, to my mind, a work of uncommon beauty. . . . I believe that *Robinson Crusoe* and *Peter Wilkins* could only have been written by islanders. No continentalist could have conceived either tale. . . . It would require a very peculiar genius to add another tale *ejusdem generis* to *Robinson Crusoe* and *Peter Wilkins*. I once projected such a thing, but the difficulty of the preoccupied ground stopped me.

[1] This Robert Paltock was the author of *Peter Wilkins*.

Perhaps La Motte Fouqué might effect something; but I should fear that neither he nor any other German could entirely understand what may be called the *desert island* feeling. I would try the marvellous line of *Peter Wilkins* if I attempted it rather than the real fiction of *Robinson Crusoe*" (*Table Talk*, 1851, pp. 331-332). Southey, in a note on a passage of the *Curse of Kehama*, went so far as to say that Paltock's winged people "are the most beautiful creatures of imagination that ever were devised," and added that Sir Walter Scott was a warm admirer of the book. With Charles Lamb at Christ's Hospital the story was a favourite. "We had classics of our own," he says, "without being beholden to 'insolent Greece or haughty Rome,' that passed current among us—*Peter Wilkins*, the *Adventures of the Hon. Captain Robert Boyle*, the *Fortunate Blue-coat Boy*, and the like." But nobody loved the old romance with such devotion as Leigh Hunt. He was never tired of discoursing about its beauties, and he wrote with such thorough appreciation of his subject that he left little or nothing for another to add. "It is interesting," he writes in one place, "to fancy R. P., or 'Mr. Robert Paltock of Clement's Inn,' a gentle lover of books, not successful enough, perhaps, as a barrister to lead a public or profitable life, but eking out a little employment or a bit of a patrimony with literature congenial to him, and looking oftener to *Purchas's Pilgrims* on his shelves than to *Coke on Littleton*. We picture him to ourselves

with *Robinson Crusoe* on one side of him and
Gaudentio di Lucca on the other, hearing the pen
go over his paper in one of those quiet rooms in
Clement's Inn that look out of its old-fashioned
buildings into the little garden with the dial in it
held by the negro: one of the prettiest corners in
London, and extremely fit for a sequestered fancy
that cannot get any farther. There he sits, the
unknown, ingenious, and amiable Mr. Robert Paltock, thinking of an imaginary beauty for want of
a better, and creating her for the delight of posterity
though his contemporaries were to know little or
nothing of her. We shall never go through the
place again without regarding him as its crowning
interest. . . . Now a sweeter creature [than You-
warkee] is not to be found in books; and she does
him immortal honour. She is all tenderness and
vivacity; all born good taste and blessed companionship. Her pleasure consists but in his; she prevents
all his wishes; has neither prudery nor immodesty;
sheds not a tear but from right feeling; is the good
of his home and the grace of his fancy. It has
been well observed that the author has not made
his flying women in general light and airy enough.
. . . And it may be said, on the other hand, that
the kind of wing, the graundee, or elastic drapery
which opens and shuts at pleasure, however ingeniously and even beautifully contrived, would neces-
sitate creatures whose modifications of humanity,
bodily and mental, though never so good after their
kind, might have startled the inventor had he been

more of a naturalist; might have developed a being very different from the feminine, sympathising, and lovely Youwarkee. Muscles and nerves not human must have been associated with inhuman wants and feelings; probably have necessitated talons and a beak! At best the woman would have been wilder, more elvish, capricious, and unaccountable. She would have ruffled her whalebones when angry; been horribly intimate, perhaps, with birds' nests and fights with eagles; and frightened Wilkins out of his wits with dashing betwixt rocks and pulling the noses of seals and gulls " (*Book for a Corner*, 1868, i. 68, etc.). Could criticism be more delightful? But in the *London Journal*, November 5th, 1834, the genial essayist's fancy dallied even more daintily with the theme: "A peacock with his plumage displayed, full of 'rainbows and starry eyes,' is a fine object, but think of a lovely woman set in front of an ethereal shell and wafted about like a Venus. . . . We are to picture to ourselves a nymph in a vest of the finest texture and most delicate carnation. On a sudden this drapery parts in two and flies back, stretched from head to foot like an oval fan or an umbrella; and the lady is in front of it, preparing to sweep blushing away from us and 'winnow the buxom air.'"

For many of us the conduct of life is becoming evermore a thing of greater perplexity. It is wearisome to be rudely jostling one another for the world's prizes, while myriads are toiling round us in an Egyptian bondage unlit by one ray of sunshine

ARTHUR HENRY BULLEN

from the candle to the grave. Some have attained
to Lucretian heights of philosophy, whence they
look with indifference over the tossing world-wide
sea of human misery; but others are fain to avert
their eyes, to clean forget for a season the actual
world and lose themselves in the mazes of romance.
In moments of despondency there is no greater
relief to a fretted spirit than to turn to the *Odyssey*
or Mr. Payne's exquisite translation of the *Arabian
Nights*. Great should be our gratitude to Mr.
Morris for teaching us in golden verse that *Love
is Enough*, and for spreading wide the gates of his
Earthly Paradise. Lucian's *True History*, that
carries us over unknown seas beyond the Atlantic
bounds to enchanted islands in the west, is one of
those books which we do not half appreciate. And
among the world's benefactors Robert Paltock deserves a place. An idle hour could not be spent
in a much pleasanter way than in watching Peter
Wilkins go a-field with his gun or haul up the
beast-fish at the lonely creek. What can be more
delightful than the description how, wakened from
dreams of home by the noise of strange voices overhead, he sees fallen at his door the lovely winged
woman Youwarkee! Prudish people may be scan-
dalised at the unreserved frankness shown in the
account of the consummation of Wilkins' marriage
with this fair creature; but the editor was unwilling to mutilate the book in the interests of such
refined readers. A man or a woman who can find
anything to shock his or her feelings in the descrip-

210

tion of Youwarkee's bridal night deserves the commiseration of sensible people. Very charming is the picture of the children sitting round the fire on the long winter evenings listening wide-eyed to the ever-fresh story of their father's marvellous adventures. The wholesome morality, the charitableness and homely pity apparent throughout, give the narrative a charm denied to many works of greater literary pretension. When Peter Wilkins leaves his solitary home to live among the winged people, the interest of the story, it must be confessed, is somewhat diminished. The author's obligations to Swift in the latter part of the book are considerable; and of course in describing how Peter Wilkins ordered his life on the lonely island, he was largely indebted to Defoe. But the creation of the winged beings is Paltock's own. It has been suggested that he named his hero after John Wilkins, Bishop of Chester, who, among other curious theories, had seriously discussed the question whether men could acquire the art of flying. In the second part of his *Mathematical Magick*, the Bishop writes: "Those things that seem very difficult and fearfull at the first may grow very facil after frequent trial and exercise: And therefore he that would effect any thing in this kind must be brought up to the constant practice of it from his Youth ; trying first only to use his wings in running on the ground, as an Estrich or tame geese will do, touching the earth with his toes; and so by degrees learn to rise higher till he shall attain unto skill and confidence. I have heard it from credible testimony that one of our nation hath proceeded so far in this experiment that he was able by the help of wings to skip constantly ten yards at a time." Youwarkee spread wide her graundee, and in an instant was lost in the clouds. Had the author given her the motion of a goose, or even of an ostrich—bah! the thought is too dreadful!

Judicious reader, when the long winter evenings come round, you have abundance of leisure. Let the poets stand idle on the shelves till the return of spring, unless perchance you would fain resume acquaintance with the *Seasons*, which you have not read since a boy, or would divert yourself with Prior or be grave with Crabbe. Now is the time to feel once more the charm of Lamb's peerless and unique essays; now is the time to listen to the honied voice of Leigh Hunt discoursing daintily of men and books. So you will pass from Charles Lamb and Leigh Hunt to the books they loved to praise. Exult in the full-blooded, bracing life which pulses in the pages of Fielding; and if Smollett's mirth is occasionally too riotous and his taste too coarse, yet confess that all faults must be pardoned to the author of *Humphry Clinker*. Many a long evening you will spend pleasantly with Defoe; and then, perchance, after a fresh reading of the thrice and four times wonderful adventures of Robinson Crusoe, you will turn to the romance of *Peter Wilkins*. So may rheums and catarrhs be far from you, and may your hearth be crowned with content!

THE SUN AND THE BROOK

By Richard Jefferies

THE sun first sees the brook in the meadow where some roach swim under a bulging root of ash. Leaning against the tree, and looking down into the water, there is a picture of the sky. Its brightness hides the sandy floor of the stream as a picture conceals the wall where it hangs, but, as if the water cooled the rays, the eye can bear to gaze on the image of the sun. Over its circle thin threads of summer cloud are drawn; it is only the reflection, yet the sun seems closer seen in the brook, more to do with us, like the grass, and the tree, and the flowing stream. In the sky it is so far, it cannot be approached, nor even gazed at, so that by the very virtue and power of its own brilliance it forces us to ignore and almost forget it. The summer days go on, and no one notices the sun. The sweet water slipping past the green flags, with every now and then a rushing sound of eager haste, receives the sky, and it becomes a part of the earth and of life. No one can see his own face without a glass; no one can sit down and deliberately think of the soul till it appears a visible thing. It eludes—the mind cannot grasp it. But hold a flower in the

213

hand—a rose, this later honeysuckle, or this the
first harebell—and in its beauty you can recognise
your own soul reflected as the sun in the brook.
For the soul finds itself in beautiful things.

Between the bulging root and the bank there is
a tiny oval pool, on the surface of which the light
does not fall. There the eye can see deep down
into the stream, which scarcely moves in the hollow
it has worn for itself as its weight swings into the
concave of the bend. The hollow is illumined by
the light which sinks through the stream outside
the root; and beneath, in the green depth, five or
six roach face the current. Every now and then a
tiny curl appears on the surface inside the root, and
must rise up to come there. Unwinding as it goes,
its raised edge lowers and becomes lost in the level.
Dark moss on the base of the ash darkens the water
under. The light green leaves overhead yield gently
to the passing air; there are but few leaves on the
tree, and these scarcely make a shadow on the grass
beyond that of the trunk. As the branch swings,
the gnats are driven farther away to avoid it.
Over the verge of the bank, bending down almost
to the root in the water, droop the heavily seeded
heads of tall grasses which, growing there, have
escaped the scythe.

These are the days of the convolvulus, of ripening
berry, and dropping nut. In the gateways, ears of
wheat hang from the hawthorn boughs, which
seized them from the passing load. The broad
aftermath is without flowers; the flowers are gone

to the uplands and the untilled wastes. Curving opposite the south, the hollow side of the brook has received the sunlight like a silvered speculum every day that the sun has shone. Since the first violet of the meadow, till now that the berries are ripening, through all the long drama of the summer, the rays have visited the stream. The long, loving touch of the sun has left some of its own mystic attraction in the brook. Resting here, and gazing down into it, thoughts and dreams come flowing as the water flows. Thoughts without words, mobile like the stream, nothing compact that can be grasped and stayed: dreams that slip silently as water slips through the fingers. The grass is not grass alone; the leaves of the ash above are not leaves only. From tree, and earth, and soft air moving, there comes an invisible touch which arranges the senses to its waves as the ripples of the lake set the sand in parallel lines. The grass sways and fans the reposing mind; the leaves sway and stroke it, till it can feel beyond itself and with them, using each grass blade, each leaf, to abstract life from earth and ether. These then become new organs, fresh nerves and veins running afar out into the field, along the winding brook, up through the leaves, bringing a larger existence. The arms of the mind open wide to the broad sky.

Some sense of the meaning of the grass, and leaves of the tree, and sweet waters hovers on the confines of thought, and seems ready to be resolved into definite form. There is a meaning in these things, a meaning in all that exists, and it comes near to declare itself. Not yet, not fully, nor in such shape that it may be formulated—if ever it will be—but sufficiently so to leave, as it were, an unwritten impression that will remain when the glamour is gone, and grass is but grass, and a tree a tree.

DR. BRANDES ON SHAKESPEARE

By William Archer

"Others abide our question—thou art free," wrote Matthew Arnold of Shakespeare, summing up in a single line the orthodox creed of English Shakespearology. We have fortified our souls in a resolute, nay, a defiant, agnosticism. We have made up our minds that nothing can and nothing shall be known about Shakespeare the man; and having, after a struggle, deliberately resigned ourselves to nescience, we are apt to regard as an impertinence any endeavour to arouse us from our "settled, low content." Dr. Georg Brandes, then, may expect to find his critical study of Shakespeare—a critical biography one might almost call it—hotly resented in several quarters. For Dr. Brandes cannot resign himself to absolute ignorance with regard to the spiritual history of " the monarch of mankind." Confronted with the enigma of Shakespeare's personality, Dr. Brandes is not content to shrug his shoulders and say, " I give it up." Shakespeare, he says, must and does " abide our question," if we put it in the true critical spirit. To the anecdote-monger, the biographical gossip, he has little enough to say, but to the psychologist he is reasonably communicative:

Far too long (says Dr. Brandes) it has been the custom to say, "We know nothing about Shakespeare," or, "An octavo page would contain all our knowledge of him." Even Swinburne has written of the intangibility of his personality in his works. Such assertions have been carried so far that a wretched group of *dilettanti* has been bold enough, in Europe and America, to deny William Shakespeare the right to his own life-work, to give to another the honour due to his genius, and to bespatter him and his invulnerable name with an insane abuse which has re-echoed through every land. . . . It is the author's opinion that, given the possession of some forty important works by any man, it is entirely our own fault if we know nothing whatever about him. The poet has incorporated his whole individuality in these writings, and there, if we can read aright, we shall find him.

This, in the eyes of many, is a damnable heresy; but Dr. Brandes is pretty well inured to the position of a heresiarch.

It must not be supposed, however, that he has any very new or subversive theory to propound. He does not profess to have made original researches or to have unearthed new facts. He has discovered no cypher and reads no esoteric meaning or message into the poet's work. The drift of his thought—as of all sane Shakespearology—is to substitute a natural for a miraculous Shakespeare. For the impersonality theory is essentially a miraculous one. It regards Shakespeare as a sort of mechanical mouthpiece, through which the Spirit of Drama chose to address the world; or, say, a "trance medium" speaking by literal, not merely figurative, inspiration. This is the only logical conclusion to be drawn from a doctrine which forbids us to seek in Shakespeare's works for any record or indication of his personal opinions, emotions, or experiences. The tacit implication is that the most vivid interpreter of emotion the world has ever seen was himself a man of highly unemotional temperament, a hard-headed, pushing business man, who happened to have a peculiar gift for making puppets dance, and used it diligently in order to fill his pockets and found a family. All that we know of artistic psychology contradicts this assumption, and forces us to substitute "miraculous" for "peculiar" in describing the postulated "gift." Genius is not the faculty of making bricks without straw, but of utilising superbly the straws provided by observation and experience. The Elizabethan Drama, be it observed, is not, like the "well-made play" of the modern French stage, an art-form which on principle excludes everything but plot, situation, and such a modicum of character as the plot absolutely necessitates. On the contrary, it is largely, one might almost say limitlessly, discursive. It is crammed with reflective and didactic matter. It habitually combines the essay, the invective, the undramatised character-study, the satirical onslaught, general or personal, the political or topical allusion, with the strictly dramatic elements of plot, situation, and character. In other words, it is not merely dramatic, but lyrical, rhetorical, and philosophical in the highest degree. Shakespeare, moreover, availed himself to the full of all the extra-dramatic opportunities offered by the form in which he worked. Is it reasonable, then, to argue that none of the lineaments of Shakespeare the man can by any possibility be discerned in the works of Shakespeare the dramatist—to say nothing of Shakespeare the sonneteer? We may surely reply, with Dr. Brandes, that it is the height of unreason. The prevalence of this view is, I think, due to two obscure causes: first, the instinct which prompts us to make Shakespeare a miracle at all hazards; second, a deep-seated resentment of the scantiness of external data as to the poet's life and character. Since Fate has played us the scurvy trick of wiping out almost all personal records, we petulantly abjure the quest for knowledge, and seek comfort in dogmatic nescience.

Even those who most deprecate Dr. Brandes's method, and who find most to criticise in the details of his work, can scarcely fail to acknowledge and admire the extraordinary grasp of mind he has shown, and his mastery of the gigantic literature of his subject. It must be remembered that every year that passes makes a large addition, if not to the difficulties, at any rate to the necessary labours, of the Shakespeare student. The task of such critics as Ulrici and Gervinus was mere child's play in comparison with that which confronted Dr. Brandes. A whole library of formal commentators has to

be read, lest here and there a gleam of light should
lurk amid much darkening of counsel; and the
far more valuable but scarcely less voluminous
records of textual criticism, and investigations of
sources, allusions, and metres, have to be mastered
and brought to bear. Dr. Brandes has shrunk
from no labour. He has sifted, one may venture
to say, the whole mass of Shakespeare criticism,
English, American, German, French, historical,
æsthetic, ethical, chronological, textual, metrical,
and even Baconian. Whatever else its value, then,
his book is a veritable encyclopædia of Shakespearean information. It is a work of well-nourished
scholarship if ever there was one. In mere bulk
it ranks among the fullest treatments of the subject; and it is not distended by windy ethical and
æsthetic sermonisings, but is at all points real and
vital, full of definite exposition and solid argument.
It may be thought that Dr. Brandes gives too much
space to historical digressions, notably to the history
of Essex and Southampton, which opens the second
book, and to the picture of crime and corruption
at the Court of James I. which serves as frontispiece to the third book. But these disquisitions
are not, in his mind, digressions at all. He holds
that the tragical result of the Essex conspiracy
contributed to the darkening of Shakespeare's
mood, which undoubtedly synchronised with it,
and that the hideous corruption of the Court of
James helped to plunge him into that abyss of
misogyny and misanthropy which he sounded in

Troilus and *Timon*. We may or may not accept the theory that political and social phenomena exercised a distinct influence on Shakespeare's mental history; but we cannot fairly blame Dr. Brandes for submitting his evidence in detail to a public which, be it remembered, is not primarily English, but European.

Dr. Brandes accepts in the main the received chronology, and the division of Shakespeare's career into four or five periods, upon which the best English critics are practically agreed. We have first the period of youthful experiment, with *A Midsummer Night's Dream* and *Romeo and Juliet* for its culminating points; then the period of serene mastery, extending (roughly speaking) from *Henry IV.* to *Twelfth Night*; then the period of tragic gloom, extending from *Julius Cæsar* to *Antony and Cleopatra*; then the aforesaid plunge into misogyny and misanthropy; and finally the Indian Summer of restored serenity, extending from *Pericles* to *The Tempest*. Trivialities apart, Dr. Brandes does not seriously differ from Professor Dowden (to name one representative critic) in his mapping out of Shakespeare's life. His originality lies (for good or ill, as the case may be) in his rebellion against the timorousness which preserves throughout an attitude of suspended judgment, and will not accept and build upon anything short of legal proof. In Dr. Brandes's view, some probabilities are so strong as to amount to practical certainties, and to justify us in making them the bases of further reasoning and generalisation. A catena of probabilities or improbabilities may be as convincing, he thinks, as a piece of direct evidence; and having once attained a positive or negative conviction on any given point, he does not hesitate to co-ordinate that conviction with others and build further upon the foundation thus secured. He holds, in short, that valuable and trustworthy results are to be obtained from the careful sifting of evidence, and he sets about the task with a diligence that is beyond praise, and in as sane a critical spirit as ever was brought to bear upon this vast and complex problem. There is a good deal of evidence yet to be brought to light, no doubt, and it will all be re-sifted many a time and oft before a final residuum is reached that shall command universal acceptance. The end is not yet, and Dr. Brandes, I am sure, would be the last to claim finality for his work. But I am much mistaken if he be not recognised by scholars of the future as one of the foremost among those who have striven in the right direction, and have substantially advanced the frontier line of knowledge.

On the whole, Dr. Brandes gives much more weight to English than to German criticism. A psychologist by taste and training, he is never led astray by German ethical and political cobweb-spinning. Sometimes, however, he gives too much attention (in my judgment) to the fantasies of German students with regard to historic parallels which may have been present to Shakespeare's mind in the composition of this or that tragedy. For instance, I find it impossible to conceive that any recollection of the Leicester-Essex scandal, or of the Darnley-Bothwell imbroglio, had the remotest influence upon the composition of *Hamlet*. Dr. Brandes, it is true, in no way builds upon these coincidences. He says:

Although there is in all this no lack of parallels to Hamlet's circumstances, it is, of course, as ridiculous to take James as to take Essex for the actual model of Hamlet. Nothing could at that time have been stupider or more tactless than to remind the heir-presumptive to the throne, or the new King, of the deplorable circumstances of his early history. This does not exclude the supposition, however, that contemporary history supplied Shakespeare with certain outward elements, which, in the moment of conception, contributed to the picture bodied forth by the creative energy of his genius.

The supposition, indeed, cannot be entirely excluded, but it is so far-fetched as to be negligible. On the other hand, Dr. Brandes deals in a masterly and convincing fashion with the theory which traces a great deal of the philosophy of *Hamlet* to the influence of Giordano Bruno. The chapter on Bruno and Montaigne is one of the ablest in the book. As regards the Sonnets, Dr. Brandes utterly rejects the Southampton theory, and accepts as fairly convincing not only the Pembroke hypothesis, but Mr. Tyler's identification of the Dark Lady with Mistress Mary Fitton. He even adopts the extravagant suggestion that the puppet-show

scene in Ben Jonson's *Bartholomew Fair* may be
an allusion to the relations of Shakespeare and
Pembroke with Mrs. Fitton; though, if we must
find personal satire in it, Aubrey's anecdote of
Beaumont and Fletcher, quoted by Dr. Brandes
himself, would afford an infinitely more probable
peg on which to hang the allusion.

Dr. Brandes's intense admiration for Shakespeare
is rendered all the more telling by the complete
independence of his attitude. He is no fanatic,
no indiscriminating adorer. Let me quote, as an
example of his criticism in the narrower sense of
the word, a passage from his chapter on *Julius
Cæsar*, in which he considers and dismisses the
reasons which have been alleged for Shakespeare's
belittling of the character of Cæsar:

Shakespeare dared not (says Gervinus) arouse too
great interest in Cæsar; he had to throw into relief
everything about him that could account for the
conspiracy; and, moreover, he had Plutarch's distinct statement that Cæsar's character had greatly
deteriorated shortly before his death. Hudson
practically agrees with this, holding that Shakespeare
wished to present Cæsar as he appeared in the eyes
of the conspirators, so that " they too might have
fair and equal judgment at our hands "; admitting,
for the rest, that " Cæsar was literally too great to
be seen by them," and that " Cæsar is far from being
himself in these scenes; hardly one of the speeches
put in his mouth can be regarded as historically
characteristic." Thus Hudson arrives at the astonishing result that " there is an undertone of irony
at work in the ordering and tempering of this composition," explaining that, " when such a shallow
idealist as Brutus is made to overtop and outshine

the greatest practical genius the world ever saw,"
we are bound to assume that the intention is ironical.

This is the emptiest cobweb-spinning. There is no
trace of irony in the representation of Brutus. Nor
can we fall back upon the argument that Cæsar,
after his death, becomes the chief personage of the
drama, and as a corpse, as a memory, as a spirit,
strikes down his murderers. How can so small a
man cast so great a shadow! Shakespeare, of course,
intended to show Cæsar as triumphing after his
death. He has changed Brutus's evil genius, which
appears to him in the camp and at Philippi, into
Cæsar's ghost; but this ghost is not sufficient to
rehabilitate Cæsar in our estimation.

Nor is it true that Cæsar's greatness would have
impaired the unity of the piece. Its poetic value,
on the contrary, suffers from his pettiness. The play
might have been immeasurably richer and deeper
than it is, had Shakespeare been inspired by a feeling
of Cæsar's greatness.

Elsewhere in Shakespeare one marvels at what
he has made out of poor and meagre material. Here,
history was so enormously rich, that his poetry has
become poor and meagre in comparison with it.

What I chiefly miss in Dr. Brandes's work is
a final chapter giving a synopsis of results, and
enabling the reader to test in close succession the
different chains of probability on which the critic's
conclusions depend. To take one example among
many: Most people would instinctively regard it
as improbable that domestic events taking place
in distant Stratford should determine Shakespeare's
choice of subjects, and that he should give direct
and immediate expression to his private sorrows
through the mouths of his dramatic characters.
But if we see good reason to believe that the death

of his son Hamnet immediately preceded the composition of *King John*, with the lamentations of Constance for her Arthur, that the death of his father immediately preceded the composition of *Hamlet*, and that the death of his mother immediately preceded the composition of *Coriolanus*, we could scarcely help finding a significance in the series of three coincidences, which it would be absurd to attach to any single one of them. I have not gone closely into the chronological evidence in these three cases. It satisfies Dr. Brandes, and that is so much in its favour. But he might have set the matter at rest by bringing the three coincidences together, and definitely summing up the probabilities. Such a conspectus of results, however, would very likely have taken up too much space. Why should not Dr. Brandes make a separate book of it, now that he has all his material ready to hand?

A CLOUD OF PINAFORES

By Max Beerbohm

THE modish appanage of Beauty in her barouche is not a spaniel, now, but a little child. The wooden wicket which, even in my day, barred the topmost of the stairs, has been taken off its hinges, and the Jewels roll down into Cornelia's drawing-room at will. Cornelia's callers are often privileged to a place at nursery-tea. The bread-and-butter is not cut thick, as in their day, and that old law, which made it precedent of cake, seems to have been rescinded. Nor is any curb set on little tongues. Cornelia and her callers grow glad in the frolic of artless *aperçus*. They are sick of *sèvres* and scandal. Only the fresh air of the nursery can brace their frail bodies and keep up their weary eyelids.

Yes! A casual optimist might proclaim that the Victorian Era is harking back to its first simplicity. At the risk of saddening him, I must suggest that he examine his opinion. I fear there are flaws in it. Between the Georgian and Victorian Eras came an interval of transition. Society was tired of its old pleasures, but did not quite abandon them. It still masked and gambled, but only a little, in a quiet way, as by force of habit. It was really

228

resting. And when William died and was succeeded by a young Queen, herself a symbol of all simplicity, it was ready for renunciation. It had regained its old strength, was strong enough to be simple. In the gradual years, after the Queen-widow had withdrawn herself, ceding the supremacy to her eldest son, Society slipped into its old ways. Surfeit came in due course. Men and women sought refuge in bizarre fashions: æstheticism, slumming, Buddhism. But now surfeit has come again. They look around. What is left to them? Simplicity! But they are tired. There is no interval for rest. Also, they are less strong physically, intellectually stronger, than were their grand-parents; not strong enough, not weak enough, to be simple. But ah! there is one thing left to them. They can, at least, contemplate simplicity. There is a nursery somewhere at the top of most houses. " Let the children be brought down to lunch! Let us have tea with the children! "

One may trace, in the evolution of modern literature, a fairly exact parallel. But the cross-lines which connect the corresponding points on either side of this parallel are uniformly oblique. It may be too much to say that Life always copies Literature, yet certainly Literature is always a little ahead of Life. Thus we find that Pre-Raphaelite poets were at work before 1880, that Sir Walter Besant, too, was already bustling about the slums, and Buddha peeping from many a first, second, and third volume. Nor did Stevenson write his *Child's*

Garden, nor Pater his *Child in the House*, to meet
a demand which was as yet uncreated; nor, indeed,
did either work attract any attention. But, now
that children are booming, the publishers and the
reviewers are all agog. Stevenson and Mr. Walter
Crane are honoured with reprints. " Mr. Pater's
most exquisite achievement is *The Child in the
House* "—" *Sentimental Tommy* is the supreme
outcome of Mr. Barrie's genius "—" Mr. Kenneth
Grahame's *Golden Age* is indeed a Golden Book."
Yes! Children are in vogue. The clear carillon
of the coral-and-bells has penetrated even to the
back-benches of the Divorce Court, and the
assiduous, unimportant authors, who sat scribbling
there, have torn up their flimsies and scuttled forth
at the summons. *Faut être dans le mouvement*,
poor creatures! For a while, they will make the
scrap-screen their background. And if their heroine
wear a pinafore, not a strange tea-gown " of some
clinging green material," and prefer jam to lauda-
num and make-believe to introspection, I, for one,
shall see nothing lamentable in the difference.
Save as a guide to tendencies of the period, such
writers do not interest me much.

I find a far subtler and more amusing guide in
a little book entitled *The Children*, and written
by a lady whose talent is pre-eminently, almost
painfully, adult. Here, indeed, is a perfect example
of our tecnolatry, our delight in the undirected
oddities of children, our wistful effort to understand them as they are. We are told of a boy who,

at the sea-side, "assumes a deep, strong, and ultra-masculine note, and a swagger in his walk, and gives himself the name of his father's tallest friend. The tone is not wholly manly; it is a tone of affairs, and withal careless; it is intended to suggest business, and also the possession of a top-hat and a pipe, and is known in the family as his 'official voice.'" How nicely sympathetic is this analysis of a mood which, in my day, was called "showing-off," and was invariably discouraged! "'Listen to him, mother,'" says a little girl, "'he's trying to talk like God. He often does.'" In the unkind 'sixties this little girl would have been sent to bed as a blasphemer. In my day, she would have been told that what she said was irreverent, and that irreverence was a very terrible thing. She "seemed thoroughly to understand the situation" is our author's comment. Indeed the modern feeling is that the child can do no wrong. Its very slips in grammar, its inconsequence, its confusion of names, are all treasured with a loving care and imbued with an exquisite significance. "A nut-brown child of five was persuading another to play. 'Oh come,' she said, 'and play with me at new maid.'" Formerly, no amount of nut-brownness would have saved her from an explanation that the game was called "old" maid; as it is, I am quite sure she was kissed for her mistake by whatever grown-up person overheard it.

Certainly, I should be the last to deprecate the vogue of children, if I were to regard it from a

selfish and superficial standpoint. For if there be
one thing which people love more than to read
about children, now, it is to read what children
write. Had I not been *parmi les jeunissimes*, I
should not have made the little success I have.
The public does not, I suppose, care greatly whether
I write well nor whether my premises and conclusions be correct. But it knows me to be a child-
author, and likes to picture me at my desk, dressed
in black velveteen, with legs dangling towards
the floor. If I filled this book with the pot-hooks
and hangers, which were, till recently, my sole
literary output, the public would be just as well
pleased. But, though this sparkling tide flows all
in my favour, I cannot quite approve of it. To me,
there seems some danger in the prevalent desire
to observe children in their quiddity, to leave them
all to their own devices and let them develop their
own natures, swiftly or slowly, at will. Perhaps I
am bigoted and old-fashioned, out of touch with
the time. But I must confess that, sometimes,
my heart does even hark back to those stern old
Georgian or Early Victorian days, when nurseries
were governed in a spirit of blind despotism.
Children were not then recognised as human
creatures. They were a race apart; savages that
must be driven from the gates; beasts to be kept
in cages; devils to whose voices one must not
listen. Indeed, the very nature of children was
held to be sinful. Lies and sloth, untidiness and
irreverence, and a tendency to steal blackcurrant

jam, were taken to be its chief constituents. And so all nurseries, as one may learn from old books or from the oral tradition, were the darkened scene of temporal oppression, fitfully lighted with the gaunt reflections of hell-fire. How strange a picture is to be found in those books of " cautionary verses for children," irrelevantly entitled *The Daisy* and *The Cowslip*. Anything less flower-like than their tone could not be easily conceived. The good children who move through their pages are the merest puppets, worked by the monstrous autocrat, Mamma, whilst the bad children, placed there as foils, are the most mechanical of drones and dunces. Never once does the authoress betray the briefest wish to treat children objectively. Yet, curious though it seem to modern ideas, she typifies the parents of her period.

Children were not neglected in those days. Their parents' sedulous endeavour was to force them up to a standard of mature conduct. They were taught that only their elders were good, and they were punished always in so far as they behaved childishly. See, even, how they were dressed! Miss Caroline, when she walked out, was framed in a crinoline, and she shaded her ringlets with a minute parasol, whilst Master Richard, her brother, in nankeen trousers, was a small replica of his papa. Later, in the 'seventies and 'eighties, before the Child, as such, was cared for, we see the little girl still tricked out in the latest fashion of maturity, and the little boy masquerading as a highlander

or as a sailor. Nowadays, they are both put into
the limpest, simplest " things." The 'nineties wish
children to be children, and nothing more. If—
to take but one of the many pregnant comparisons
suggested by *The Daisy* or *The Cowslip*—a little
girl of this period be suffering toothache, she is
coaxed, by all manner of sweet means, to the
dentist's chair. Her fears could not anger any one.
She is a child. But read the " cautionary verses "
about two sisters, Miss Clara and Miss Sophie,
who " both had faded teeth." Miss Clara, like
a good grown-up lady, realised that a short wrench
were as nothing to such prolonged agony. Miss
Sophie held back, trembling. No one reasoned
with her. She was suffered to be a foil to the adult
fortitude of her sister, whose

> teeth returned quite fresh and bright,
> Whilst Sophie's ached both day and night.

These are a type of the verses that were written
for children of the last generation, as *The Fairchild
Family* is a type of the prose. Even in books like
Struwelpeter the elements of terror were lurking
everywhere. When children came into the scheme
of a novel, they were, with few exceptions, prigs
like Little Nell and Paul Dombey; dreary ab-
stractions, foredoomed to the earliest of death-
beds. In fact, real children were pariahs. That,
you will say, was horrible and inhuman of their
elders. It was. But I am inclined to think that,
for the children themselves, it was a far more

wholesome state of things. For the inherent nature of childhood is far brighter than the inherent nature of maturity. Childhood has no alien responsibilities, it is free from all the bitterness of knowledge and of memory, is careless and hopeful. So that, if the nursery be turned into a free republic and be rid of its old gloom and vigilant authority, it must be the scene of absolute happiness, and its children, when the time comes for them to leave it, will be appalled by the serious side of life. Finding no pleasure in a freedom which they have always had, incapable of that self-control which long discipline produces, they will become neurotic, ineffectual men and women. In the old days there could have been no reaction of this kind. The strange sense of freedom was a recompense for less happiness of heart. Children were fit for life.

Even from the standpoint of those elders, to whose jaded longing for simplicity the new form of education must be traced, there is great reason for misgiving. For it is probable that the effort to keep children simple by leaving them free, will but exterminate simplicity, at last. It is only oppression that can keep human beings as they are. Oppression never crushes natural instincts. All history proves that it does but intensify them. Wronged races are always primitive. Left to themselves, they develop. If Home Rule were granted, the Irish would soon lose their irresponsible gaiety, which centuries of oppression have preserved for them. Indeed, that is perhaps the most valid argument against Home Rule. Miss Caroline, likewise, and Master Richard, driven to bay by their elders, set their back against the nursery wall and were simple to the last. But Jock and Millicent, encouraged in all their childishness, having but their own natures to think of, will very soon become self-conscious. "Whenever I can't stop laughing I have only to think of home." These words were written by a little boy from his first boarding-school, and are quoted in *The Children*. So you see that introspection has set in already, and soon every high-chair will hold its lisping Rousseau or Marie Bashkirtseff. And soon there will be no more simplicity to contemplate. And what will a jaded world, straining at its tether, do then? Personally I should like to think that this passion for simplicity was the sign of a lessening complexity. But wishes beget poor thoughts. I write what I believe to be true about this Victorian era. Good has been followed by evil, evil by the love of mysteries, the love of mysteries by the love of simple things. Observe that I write no fool's prattle about *la fin du siècle*. A phase of social evolution happens to coincide with a certain point in the kalendar. That, of course, is a mere chance. But we may be allowed to laugh, when we see that this century, for which Science promised a mature perfection, is vanishing in a white cloud of pinafores.

EVELYN'S DIARY

By G. W. E. Russell

"I HAVE ventured to depict the Cavalier as not invariably a drunken brute, and spiritual life and growth as not exclusively the possession of Puritans and Ascetics."

This is the account which the late J. H. Short-house gave of his own handiwork in *John Inglesant*, and there is good reason to suppose that many of its most characteristic touches were drawn from the *Diary of John Evelyn*. There is no need to restate the chronology of Evelyn's life, or the history of his family, or the circumstances under which his Diary was written. My endeavour is only to bring into prominence some personal traits, as they appear in a narrative singularly free from artifice and self-consciousness, and to trace in them the better elements which went to compose the character of the ideal Cavalier.

Let us look into Evelyn's Diary, and compare the presentment with the reality.

Nothing is more conspicuous in Evelyn than his dislike of debauchery. In this he is consistent from first to last. In 1641, when he was not quite twenty-one, we find him dining with a cavalry mess, and recording next day that "there was very good cheere, but hot service for a young drinker as I then was." In his "Greate Climacterical," he "stole away and left the companie" when he suspected that a dinner given by the Swedish Minister was to end in a debauch. The bibulous housekeeping of a "humourous old knight" he pronounces "barbarous, and much unbecoming a knight, still lesse a Christian"; and in another place he reprehends "the barbarous custom of making the masters welcome by intoxicating the servants." He commends "Mr. Garmus, the Resident from Hamburgh," because, though "his feast continu'd neere 9 whole hours," there was "no greate excess of drinking, no man being obliged to take more than he liked."

But drunkenness was by no means the only offence which disgusted him. He trounces with equal severity all the fashionable vices, and "rude and dirty pastimes." Cock-fighting, dog-fighting, and bull-baiting he pronounced "butcherly sports, or rather barbarous cruelties"; and, when "a very gallant horse was baited to death with doggs," he urged that "this wicked and barbarous sport deserv'd to have ben punish'd in the cruel contrivers." It "afflicted him to see how the Stage was degenerated and polluted by the licentious times." He found "the Revells at the Middle Temple an old and but riotous custome, which had relation neither to virtue nor policy." The banter of the "*Terræ Filius*, or Universitie Buffoon," at Oxford struck

him as "licentious lyeing, railing, and ribauldry."
"In my life I was never witnesse of so shamefull
entertainment." The vicious habits of the Court
he condemned as unsparingly as those of social and
academic life.

Evelyn was, in all the best senses of the word,
a Cavalier—a *preux chevalier*, a loyal subject of the
King, a dutiful and devoted son of the English
Church, an accomplished and high-minded gentleman, as conspicuous for purity as for all other
manly virtues. Yet, though virtuous, he was no
Puritan. The peculiar charm of the better sort of
Cavalier was that, at a period when one half of
England was debauched and the other fanatical, he
accepted culture and beauty and refinement and
enjoyment as divine gifts, and, in St. Paul's phrase,
used the world as not abusing it. Such pre-eminently
was Evelyn's mode of life, as set before us in his
minute but unstudied Diary.

A strain of innocent gaiety and refined enjoyment marks Evelyn's life from first to last. He
was born of good family in a comfortable home,
and brought up by a "too indulgent Grandmother."
He persuaded his father to spare him "the severe
discipline of Eaton," and his schooldays were spent
at Lewes and Southover—"which perverseness he
a thousand times deplored." He seems to have been
a thoroughly idle boy; but he must have had the
substantial virtues of the schoolboy's character, for,
thirty years later, he felt that he could trust his life
to a schoolfellow's loyalty. He plotted with Colonel

Morley, the Lieutenant of the Tower, for the restoration of Charles II., relying on the fact that "the Coll. had ben my schoolfellow, and I knew would not betray me." At seventeen he went up as a "fellow communer" to Balliol, having been entered at the Middle Temple in the previous year. He spent three years at Oxford, and did not over-work himself. He "was admitted into the dauncing and vaulting schole," and began to indulge that love of "musiq" and "musitians" which contributed so much to the enjoyment of his life. But from music, as from severer studies, he was "frequently diverted by inclinations to newer trifles." At twenty he came to live in London, in order that he might read law at the Middle Temple, but he had no taste for "that impolish'd study," and spent his time in "studying a little, but dancing and fooling more." As years went on, he became a man of affairs, an important member of what we should now call the Permanent Civil Service, an industrious and well-paid servant of the Crown and the nation; but neither the cares of public business, nor the stupendous events of the time, nor sorrows in his family, nor vicissitudes in his fortune, ever inclined him to a dismal view of life, or crushed his faculty of innocent enjoyment. He was, for his time, a prodigious traveller, both in England and on the Continent; and wherever he journeyed, even though his path was often beset with political and physical perils, he carried with him the same lively appreciation of all that was gay and good and beautiful. He is travelling with a friend in France, and at Rohan "they indulge themselves with the best that all France affords," so that "their supper might have satisfied a Prince." "We lay that night in damask beds, and were treated like Emperoors." Next day they resume their journey. "Sometimes we footed it thro' pleasant fields and meadows; sometimes we shot at fowls and other birds, nothing came amiss; sometimes we play'd at cards, while others sung or were composing verses." In Italy these jocund wayfarers "bought for winter provision 3000 lb. weight of excellent grapes, and pressed their owne wine, which proved incomparable liquor." But, on the ensuing Twelfth Night, they "invited all the English and Scotch in Padua to a feast, which sank our excellent wine considerably." The host was in turn a guest, and at Venice "was invited to excellent English potted venison." Returning to England, he amused himself at "Bristoll" with a "collation of fried eggs, and excellent Spanish wine." At a dinner at Blackwall he drank some "canarie incomparably good." When he dined with the Governor of the Isle of Wight, he noted the "excellent venison, fowle, fish and fruit." When one of his friends was raised to the episcopate, he enjoyed with equal zest the Service of Consecration in the Abbey, and, after it, "one of the most plentifull and magnificent dinners that in my life I ever saw—it cost neare 600l. as I was inform'd." But no partiality of friendship blinded him to the demerits of home-made wine.

" I drank of the wine of Col. Blount's vineyard, which was good for little."

Still, after all, life has other enjoyments besides the pleasures of the palate, and, as long as they were innocent, our Cavalier appreciated them all. He loved "a Consort of Musiq," both vocal and instrumental; he loved portraiture and " Mezzo Tinto " and "landskip "; he loved architecture, both classical and " gotiq." He loved the "Theater," and lamented that it was "abused to an atheistical liberty." He had a keen eye for the beauties of scenery, and, as his delightful *Sylva* shows, was an enthusiast for gardening and forestry. He was a good horseman and an admirer of horsemanship in others. He played " Mall." He could row, on occasion, for " twenty leagues." He liked shooting, hawking, and "hunting a fat buck," a "sorel deer," or even "an hare from my Lord's hare-warren." He did not disdain a bowling-match, a wrestling-match, a boat-race, or a horse-race; and he was a critical observer of a " Ball or Masque." After dinner at a friend's house, where "one Carew play'd incomparably on the Welsh harp," he "treated divers Ladies of my relations, in Spring Gardens."

But here we must turn to the second part of the text which I took from Mr. Shorthouse — "Spiritual life and growth [were] not exclusively the possession of Puritans and Ascetics." We have seen that John Evelyn was no ascetic, as regards the legitimate pleasures of human life. He was as

242

far removed from the temper of Puritanism as from that licentiousness which is sometimes supposed to be its only alternative. Yet not Baxter or Calamy, or the best Puritan of them all, was more consistently and conspicuously a Christian in faith, speech, and act.

His belief in the Church was no mere matter of theory; it was in the highest degree practical, intimate, and methodical. Nothing in his Diary is more noticeable than his devotion to the Blessed Sacrament—his strictness in preparing for it, his thankfulness for being allowed to receive it, his grief when it is withheld. He auspicates every work of special importance or peril by receiving it. When he recovers from sickness, or experiences any other signal mercy, he makes it, in the strictest sense, his "Eucharist." In order to regulate his spiritual life more exactly, he made Jeremy Taylor his "ghostly father." He ended each year and began the next with special offices of devotion. He commemorated with religious observances his birthday and the anniversary of his baptism. He was scrupulous in keeping the Church's feasts and "the Holy Weeke," and, when such observances were forbidden, under civil penalties, by triumphant Puritanism, he procured "orthodox sequestred Divines" to preach and celebrate privately in his library.

All the outward pomp and circumstance of worship was dear to him. Whether at home or abroad, he never failed to notice the decoration and equipment of the churches. He observed and described altars, vestments, pictures, sacramental plate, the "chrystal vessels" in a foreign sacristy, and the incense burnt before the Communion Service in the Chapel Royal at Whitehall. After all the alluring splendours of French and Roman worship, he returns with devout complacency to St. James's Church, in "Piqudillo." "There was no altar anywhere in England, nor has there been any abroad, more handsomely adorn'd."

But the best of friends must part, and it is time to take our leave of this devout and high-souled Cavalier. Through a long, prosperous, and enjoyable life he dwelt habitually in the thought of the final parting, and a fragment from his self-communings on that transcendent theme may not unfitly close this essay:

"I now (1682) began to looke over and methodize all my writings, accompts, letters, papers; inventoried the goods, and other articles of the house, and put things into the best order I could, and made my will; that now growing in yeares, I might have none of these secular things and concerns to distract me when it should please God to call me from this transitory life. With this I prepar'd some special meditations and devotions for the time of sickness. The Lord Jesus grant them to be salutary for my poore soul in that day, that I may obtain mercy and acceptance."

PRINTED BY
THE TEMPLE PRESS AT LETCHWORTH
IN GREAT BRITAIN